MT. PLEASANT LIBRARY
PLEASANTVILLE, NY

W9-AHL-111

Betty Crocker
Christmas
COOKIES

Houghton Mifflin Harcourt
Boston • New York • 2013

GENERAL MILLS

Food Content and Relationship Marketing Director: Geoff Johnson

Food Content Marketing Manager: Susan Klobuchar

Senior Editor: Grace Wells

Kitchen Manager: Ann Stuart

Recipe Development and Testing: Betty Crocker Kitchens

Photography: General Mills Photography Studios and Image Library

HOUGHTON MIFFLIN HARCOURT

Publisher: Natalie Chapman

Editorial Director: Cindy Kitchel

Executive Editor: Anne Ficklen

Associate Editor: Heather Dabah

Managing Editor: Marina Padakis

Production Editor: Jamie Selzer

Art Director and Book Design: Tai Blanche

Interior Layout: Eugenie S. Delaney

Production Manager: Kevin Watt

Copyright © 2013 by General Mills, Minneapolis, Minnesota. All rights reserved.

For information about permission to reproduce selections from this book, write to Permissions, Houghton Mifflin Harcourt Publishing Company, 215 Park Avenue South, New York, New York 10003.

The HERSHEY'S® KISSES® trademark and trade dress and the Conical figure and plume device are used under license.

www.hmhbooks.com

Library of Congress Cataloging-in-Publication Data is available upon request.

ISBN: 978-0-544-16664-6 (pbk.); 978-0-544-28819-5 (ebk.)

Manufactured in the United States of America

DOC 10 9 8 7 6 5 4 3 2 1

Cover photos (clockwise): Gingersnap Sandwich Cookies (page 46), Sugar Cookie Presents (page 64), Strawberry Cheesecake Bars (page 172), Raspberry Poinsettia Blossoms (page 98) and Chocolate Peppermint Tartlets (page 28).

The Betty Crocker Kitchens seal guarantees success in your kitchen. Every recipe has been tested in America's Most Trusted Kitchens™ to meet our high standards of reliability, easy preparation and great taste.

FIND MORE GREAT IDEAS AT

BettyCrocker.com

Dear Friends,

When Christmas comes around, it's time to start baking, and there are no better sweet treats to make than cookies, bars and brownies. They're wonderful for holiday entertaining, great as gifts and simple to bake, and they make the house smell delicious. So use these recipes to start the season off right!

All your favorites are here—enjoy Easy Spritz Cookies, Holiday Eggnog Bars, Cardamom Sugar Crisps—and more. Looking for new ideas to elevate your holiday baking? You'll love Reindeer Peanut Butter Pops, Almond Angel Cookies, Peppermint Patty Brownies and Whoopie Pies. Plus, there are even gluten-free and fun-for-kids recipes to choose from—look for the icons to find them easily.

We also included fun ideas for wrapping and packaging your baked gifts, as well as information on how to decorate your holiday goodies so that they'll be treasured by family and friends. From clever cutouts to the easiest drop cookies that are perfect for when you're short on time, all the best Christmas cookies are right here. Happy baking and happy holidays!

Sincerely,

Betty Crocker

Contents

Cookie Success Secrets

What could be better than freshly baked homemade cookies? With the tips and tricks you'll learn here, you'll be baking them up in no time.

Use the Right Ingredients

- **Flours:** Stick to bleached or unbleached all-purpose flour for cookies. Whole wheat flour can also be used, but only substitute it for one-third to one-half the amount of all-purpose flour called for in the recipe to prevent the cookies from becoming too dry. Don't use bread and cake flours when making cookies. Bread flour causes them to be tough, and cake flour causes them to be too delicate and fragile.

- **Sweeteners:** In addition to adding sweetness to cookies, sweeteners also help brown and add tenderness to baked goods. Most recipes call for granulated white sugar or brown sugar or both, but other types of sweeteners like honey or maple syrup are used in specific recipes.

- **Leavenings:** Cookies usually call for baking soda and/or baking powder. They are not interchangeable, so be sure to use what your recipe calls for.

- **Fats and Oils:** Fats add tenderness and flavor to cookies. For best results, use butter or, if the recipe calls for it, shortening. If you choose to use margarine, use only products with at least 65% fat. Any other spreads or reduced-fat products contain more water, resulting in cookies that are too soft, tough and puffy.

- **Eggs:** Eggs add richness, moisture and structure to cookies. All the recipes in this book have been tested with large eggs. Egg product substitutes, made of egg whites, can be substituted for whole eggs, but the baked cookies and bars may have a drier texture.

- **Liquids:** Liquids like water, fruit juice, milk or cream tend to make cookies crisper by causing them to spread more. Add only as much liquid as the recipe calls for.

- **Oats:** Quick-cooking and old-fashioned oats are interchangeable unless a recipe calls for a specific type. Instant oatmeal products contain other ingredients and flavors, so they should not be used as a substitute for oats in cookie recipes.

- **Nuts and Peanuts:** When nuts are called for in a recipe, you can substitute any variety of nut or peanuts. Nuts can become rancid, giving them an unpleasant, strong flavor that can ruin the taste of cookies. Always taste these items before adding them to a recipe; if they don't taste fresh, throw them out.

Softening Butter

The best way to soften butter is to leave it at room temperature 30 to 45 minutes because it will soften evenly. To soften it in the microwave, remove the foil or waxed wrapper. Place butter in a microwavable bowl, uncovered. Microwave ½ to 1 cup butter on High 15 to 30 seconds.

Choose Your Cookie Sheets Wisely

Choosing the right cookie sheet can make all the difference in how your cookies bake up.

- A cookie sheet is a flat pan that may be open on one to three sides. If the sheet has four sides, cookies may not brown as evenly.

- Cookie sheets come in three basic types. Here's how cookies bake on each type:

  - **Shiny Aluminum with Smooth Surface:** These are the top choice for cookie bakers. They reflect heat, allowing cookies to bake evenly and brown properly. The recipes in this book were tested using these cookie sheets.

  - **Insulated:** These sheets help prevent cookies from turning too dark on the bottom. Cookies baked on these sheets may take longer to bake; the bottoms will be light colored, and the cookies may not brown as much overall. They may be difficult to remove from these sheets because the bottoms of the cookies are more tender.

- **Nonstick and Dark-Surface:** Cookies baked on these sheets may be smaller in diameter and more rounded. The tops and especially the bottoms will be more browned, and the bottoms may be hard. Check cookies at the minimum bake time so they don't get too brown or burn. Follow the manufacturer's directions; some recommend reducing the oven temperature by 25°F.

- Choose sheets that are at least 2 inches smaller (on all sides) than the inside of your oven to allow heat to circulate.

- Have at least two cookie sheets so that while one batch is baking you're getting the next batch ready to go into the oven.

Bake a Test Cookie

Make sure your cookies will turn out perfectly by baking one cookie as a test first, to see the shape of the cookie before you commit to baking any more. That way, you can make adjustments to the dough before baking the rest of the batch.

- If the test cookie spreads too much, add 1 to 2 tablespoons flour to the dough.

- If the test cookie is too round or hard, add 1 to 2 tablespoons milk to the dough.

Top Tips for Perfect Cookies

1. Use completely cooled cookie sheets. Cookies will spread too much on sheets that are still warm.

2. Make cookies all the same size so they bake evenly. Spring-handled cookie or ice-cream scoops make evenly portioning the dough a breeze. Measure the volume of the scoop with water first to make sure it's the size your cookie recipe says to portion the dough by.

3. Bake cookies on the middle oven rack. For even baking, it's best to bake one sheet at a time. If you do bake two sheets at once, position the oven racks as close to the middle as possible and switch sheets halfway through baking.

4. Check cookies at the minimum bake time and bake longer only if needed.

5. Many cookies benefit by cooling on the cookie sheet a minute or two so they firm up and are easier to remove from the sheet.

6. Remove cookies from the cookie sheet using a flat, thin metal spatula. Cool as directed.

7. If cookies were left too long on the cookie sheet and are difficult to remove, put the cookies back into the oven for 1 to 2 minutes, and then remove them from the sheet. They should come off easily.

Storing Cookies and Bars

- **Crisp Cookies:** Store at room temperature in loosely covered containers.

- **Soft and Chewy Cookies:** Store at room temperature in resealable food-storage plastic bags or tightly covered containers.

- **Both Types of Cookies:** Keep crisp cookies from becoming soft by storing them separately from soft, chewy cookies.

- **Frosted or Decorated Cookies:** Let cookies harden before storing. Place between layers of cooking parchment or waxed paper, plastic wrap or foil.

- **Flavored Cookies:** Use separate containers to store different-flavored cookies to prevent them from picking up flavors from the other cookies.

- **Bars:** Follow directions in specific bar recipes for the correct storage. Most can be tightly covered, but some may be loosely covered or refrigerated.

- **Freezing Cookies and Bars:** Tightly wrap completely cooled cookies and bars, and label them. Freeze unfrosted cookies up to 1 year and frosted/decorated cookies up to 3 months. Place them in single layers in freezer containers, and cover with waxed paper before adding another layer. Do not freeze meringue, custard-filled or cream-filled cookies.

Bar and Brownie Success Secrets

For bars and brownies to turn out perfectly every time, it's all about the pan you use and tips for cutting them.

Choose the Right Pan

Use the exact size of pan called for in the recipe when baking bars or brownies. If made in too big of a pan, bars will be hard and overbaked. Bars made in pans that are too small can be doughy in the center and have hard edges.

Shiny metal pans are recommended for baking bars. They reflect heat and prevent the bottom from getting too brown and hard. Check bars at the minimum bake time and bake longer only if needed.

Follow the manufacturer's directions when using dark, nonstick or glass baking pans; they may recommend reducing the oven temperature by 25°F. Check for doneness 3 to 5 minutes before the minimum bake time given in the recipe.

Cutting Bars and Brownies Perfectly

- **Line the Pan:** Lining the pan with foil before baking makes it easy to cut bars and brownies—and is great for quick cleanup! Turn the pan upside down. Tear off a piece of foil longer than the pan. Smooth the foil around the pan bottom and sides and then remove. Flip the pan over, and gently fit the shaped foil into the pan. When the bars or brownies are cool, lift them out of the pan using the edges of foil as handles. Peel back the foil and cut the bars or brownies as directed.

- **Use a Plastic Knife:** Our food stylists have found that plastic knives work best for cutting brownies and soft, sticky bars such as Mint Cheesecake Squares (page 190). They also prevent your pans from getting scratched, as they could if you use a metal knife.

chapter one

Fun & Filled

Caramel-Filled Sandies

PREP TIME: **40 Minutes** • START TO FINISH: **1 Hour 5 Minutes** • **3 dozen cookies**

COOKIES

- 1 pouch Betty Crocker® sugar cookie mix
- ¼ cup finely chopped toasted pecans*
- 2 tablespoons all-purpose flour
- ½ cup butter, softened
- 1 egg

FILLING AND GARNISH

- 34 caramel candies, unwrapped (from 14-oz bag)
- 3 tablespoons half-and-half
- ⅓ cup dark chocolate chips, melted
- ⅓ cup white baking chips, melted
- 1 tablespoon coarse sea salt

1. Heat oven to 375°F. In medium bowl, combine cookie mix, pecans, flour, butter and egg until soft dough forms. Shape into 1½-inch balls. On ungreased cookie sheets, place balls 2 inches apart. Using thumb or handle of wooden spoon, make indentation in center of each cookie.

2. Bake 8 to 10 minutes or until edges are light golden brown. Cool; remove from cookie sheets to cooling racks. Cool completely, about 15 minutes.

3. In small microwavable bowl, microwave caramels and half-and-half uncovered on High 1 to 2 minutes, stirring once, until caramels are melted. Spoon 1 teaspoon caramel into indentation of each cookie. Cool 15 minutes.

4. Drizzle with melted dark chocolate and white baking chips. Sprinkle with salt. Let stand 15 minutes or until chocolate is set.

To toast pecans, bake in ungreased shallow pan at 350°F for 5 to 8 minutes, stirring occasionally, until light brown.

1 Cookie: Calories 150; Total Fat 7g (Saturated Fat 3g, Trans Fat 0.5g); Cholesterol 15mg; Sodium 280mg; Total Carbohydrate 21g (Dietary Fiber 0g); Protein 1g **Exchanges:** ½ Starch, 1 Other Carbohydrate, 1 Fat **Carbohydrate Choices:** 1½

Holiday Surprise Sugar Cookies

PREP TIME: **1 Hour 15 Minutes** • START TO FINISH: **1 Hour 45 Minutes** • **4 dozen cookies**

1 pouch Betty Crocker sugar cookie mix

⅓ cup butter, softened

1 egg

2 tablespoons all-purpose flour

Red and green food colors

16 thin rectangular crème de menthe candies, cut into thirds

Assorted colored candy sprinkles, sugars, decors and decorating gels

1. Heat oven to 375°F. In medium bowl, stir cookie mix, butter, egg and flour until dough forms. Divide dough into thirds. Tint one-third red and one-third green with food colors; leave one-third plain. Keep dough covered tightly until ready to use.

2. On floured surface, roll each third of dough to ⅛-inch thickness. For round cookies, cut with 1½-inch cookie cutter; for square cookies, cut into 1½-inch squares using sharp knife. (Dip cutter or knife in flour for easier cutting.)

3. On ungreased cookie sheet, place half the cookies 1 inch apart. Place 1 candy piece on center of each cookie; top with another cookie. Gently press edges together to seal, using tines of fork. To decorate before baking, sprinkle cookies with sprinkles, sugars or decors as desired.

4. Bake 6 to 8 minutes or until edges are light brown. Cool 1 minute; remove from cookie sheet to cooling rack. Cool completely, about 30 minutes. Decorate with gels as desired.

1 Cookie: Calories 70; Total Fat 3.5g (Saturated Fat 1.5g, Trans Fat 0g); Cholesterol 10mg; Sodium 35mg; Total Carbohydrate 10g (Dietary Fiber 0g); Protein 0g **Exchanges:** ½ Other Carbohydrate, 1 Fat **Carbohydrate Choices:** ½

Tinsel Time Tip

Instead of the crème de menthe candies, use one of the following in each cookie:

• Piece of a 1.55-ounce milk chocolate candy bar, separated into small rectangles, each cut into thirds (larger baking or candy bars will be too thick)

• ¼ teaspoon toffee bits

Espresso Thumbprint Cookies

PREP TIME: **1 Hour** • START TO FINISH: **1 Hour 15 Minutes** • **3½ dozen cookies**

COOKIES

¾   cup sugar

¾   cup butter, softened

½   teaspoon vanilla

1   egg

1¾   cups all-purpose flour

3   tablespoons unsweetened baking cocoa

¼   teaspoon salt

FILLING

¼   cup whipping cream

2   teaspoons instant espresso coffee granules

1   cup milk chocolate chips

1   tablespoon coffee-flavored liqueur, if desired

TOPPING

Crushed hard peppermint candies, if desired

1. Heat oven to 350°F. In large bowl, beat sugar, butter, vanilla and egg with electric mixer on medium speed, or mix with spoon, until well blended. Stir in flour, cocoa and salt until dough forms.

2. Shape dough by rounded teaspoonfuls into 42 (1-inch) balls. On ungreased cookie sheets, place balls about 2 inches apart. Using thumb or end of wooden spoon, make indentation in center of each cookie, but do not press all the way to cookie sheet.

3. Bake 7 to 11 minutes or until edges are firm. If necessary, quickly remake indentations with end of wooden spoon. Immediately remove from cookie sheets to cooling racks. Cool completely, about 30 minutes.

4. Meanwhile, in 1-quart saucepan, mix whipping cream and instant coffee. Heat over medium heat, stirring occasionally, until steaming and coffee is dissolved. Remove from heat; stir in chocolate chips until melted. Stir in liqueur. Cool about 10 minutes or until thickened.

5. Spoon rounded ½ teaspoon espresso filling into indentation in each cookie. Top with crushed candies.

1 Cookie: Calories 90; Total Fat 5g (Saturated Fat 3.5g, Trans Fat 0g); Cholesterol 15mg; Sodium 45mg; Total Carbohydrate 10g (Dietary Fiber 0g); Protein 1g **Exchanges:** ½ Starch, 1 Fat **Carbohydrate Choices:** ½

Citrus-Kissed Fig Thumbprints

1   pouch Betty Crocker sugar cookie mix

3   tablespoons all-purpose flour

½   cup butter, melted

1   teaspoon grated lemon peel

1   teaspoon grated orange peel

½   teaspoon vanilla

1   egg

⅓   cup fig preserves

1   teaspoon coarse sugar, if desired

1. Heat oven to 375°F. In medium bowl, mix cookie mix, flour, melted butter, lemon peel, orange peel, vanilla and egg until soft dough forms.

2. Shape dough into 48 (1-inch) balls. On ungreased cookie sheet, place balls 2 inches apart. Using thumb or handle of wooden spoon, make indentation in center of each cookie. Spoon about ¼ teaspoon preserves into each indentation.

3. Bake 7 to 9 minutes. Cool 2 minutes; remove from cookie sheet to cooling rack. Sprinkle with coarse sugar. Cool completely. Store tightly covered at room temperature.

1 Cookie: Calories 70; Total Fat 3g (Saturated Fat 1.5g, Trans Fat 0g); Cholesterol 10mg; Sodium 45mg; Total Carbohydrate 10g (Dietary Fiber 0g); Protein 0g **Exchanges:** ½ Other Carbohydrate, ½ Fat **Carbohydrate Choices:** ½

Lime-Kissed Cherry Thumbprints: Substitute lime peel for lemon peel and omit orange peel in step 1. In step 2, spoon ¼ teaspoon cherry preserves into each cookie indentation instead of fig preserves.

Raspberry-Pistachio Thumbprints

1   cup butter, softened

½   cup powdered sugar

2   cups all-purpose flour

1   cup finely chopped roasted pistachio nuts

1   teaspoon vanilla

¼   teaspoon salt

1   jar (12 oz) red raspberry jam

2   tablespoons powdered sugar

1. Heat oven to 325°F. In large bowl, beat butter and ½ cup powdered sugar with electric mixer on medium speed until creamy. Stir in flour, nuts, vanilla and salt.

2. Shape dough into 42 (1¼-inch) balls. On ungreased cookie sheets, place balls 1 inch apart. Using thumb or handle of wooden spoon, make indentation in center of each cookie, but do not press all the way to the cookie sheet.

3. Bake 15 to 17 minutes or until edges are set. If necessary, quickly remake indentations with end of wooden spoon handle. Remove from cookie sheets to cooling racks. Cool completely, about 30 minutes.

4. Fill each thumbprint with 1 rounded teaspoonful of the jam. Sprinkle 2 tablespoons powdered sugar over jam-filled centers.

1 Cookie: Calories 110; Total Fat 6g (Saturated Fat 3g, Trans Fat 0g); Cholesterol 10mg; Sodium 60mg; Total Carbohydrate 13g (Dietary Fiber 0g); Protein 1g **Exchanges:** ½ Starch, ½ Other Carbohydrate, 1 Fat **Carbohydrate Choices:** 1

Tinsel Time Tips

A food processor works great for finely chopping the pistachio nuts.

You can substitute strawberry jam or another favorite flavor for the raspberry jam.

Raspberry Ribbon Slices

PREP TIME: **30 Minutes** • START TO FINISH: **1 Hour** • **3 dozen cookies**

1 pouch Betty Crocker sugar cookie mix

   Butter and egg called for on cookie mix pouch

3 tablespoons all-purpose flour

4 tablespoons seedless raspberry or apricot jam (or desired flavor)

¾ cup powdered sugar

2 to 3 teaspoons milk

1. Heat oven to 375°F. In large bowl, mix cookie dough as directed on package, using butter and egg and adding flour; stir until well blended. Divide dough into thirds. Shape each third into 12-inch log. On ungreased cookie sheet, place 2 of the logs 3 inches apart; place third log on separate ungreased cookie sheet.

2. Bake 15 to 18 minutes or until edges are lightly browned. Cool 5 minutes.

3. Using handle of wooden spoon, make indentation about ½ inch wide and ¼ inch deep lengthwise down center of each log. Fill indentation on each log with 1 generous tablespoon jam. Remove from cookie sheets to cooling racks. Cool completely, about 30 minutes.

4. In small bowl, mix powdered sugar and enough of the milk until glaze is smooth and thin enough to drizzle. Drizzle over logs. Cut each log into 12 slices.

1 Cookie: Calories 100; Total Fat 4g (Saturated Fat 2g, Trans Fat 0.5g); Cholesterol 15mg; Sodium 60mg; Total Carbohydrate 15g (Dietary Fiber 0g); Protein 0g **Exchanges:** 1 Other Carbohydrate, 1 Fat **Carbohydrate Choices:** 1

Cherry-Topped Chocolate Tassies

PREP TIME: **25 Minutes** • START TO FINISH: **1 Hour 10 Minutes** • **2 dozen cookies**

½ cup butter, softened

1 package (3 oz) cream cheese, softened

1 cup all-purpose flour

⅛ teaspoon salt

1 cup miniature semisweet chocolate chips

24 large maraschino cherries, drained

1. Heat oven to 350°F. Spray 24 mini muffin cups with cooking spray.

2. In medium bowl, beat butter and cream cheese with electric mixer on medium speed until well mixed. On low speed, beat in flour and salt until dough forms.

3. Shape dough into 24 (1¼-inch) balls. Press 1 ball in bottom and up side of each muffin cup. Fill each cup with about 2 teaspoons chocolate chips. Top each with 1 cherry.

4. Bake 13 to 16 minutes or until edges are golden brown. Cool 10 minutes. Remove from muffin cups to cooling rack; cool completely.

1 Cookie: Calories 110; Total Fat 7g (Saturated Fat 4.5g, Trans Fat 0g); Cholesterol 15mg; Sodium 50mg; Total Carbohydrate 10g (Dietary Fiber 0g); Protein 1g **Exchanges:** ½ Other Carbohydrate, 1½ Fat **Carbohydrate Choices:** ½

Tinsel Time Tips

These tassies are fragile when they're hot, so it's important to let them cool 10 minutes before removing from the muffin cups. They set up once they're cooled.

Sprinkle the cookie edges while they're still hot with powdered sugar or red decorator sugar.

Peppermint Candy Tartlets

PREP TIME: **1 Hour 15 Minutes** • START TO FINISH: **1 Hour 30 Minutes** • **32 tartlets**

TART SHELLS

½	cup granulated sugar
½	cup butter, softened
½	teaspoon peppermint extract
1	egg
1½	cups all-purpose flour
¼	teaspoon baking soda
¼	teaspoon salt

FILLING AND GARNISH

2	cups powdered sugar
3	tablespoons butter, softened
2	to 3 drops red food color
2	to 3 tablespoons milk
½	cup crushed hard peppermint candies

1. Heat oven to 350°F. Grease bottoms only of 32 mini muffin cups with shortening.

2. In large bowl, beat granulated sugar and ½ cup butter with electric mixer on medium speed until fluffy. Beat in peppermint extract and egg until blended. On low speed, beat in flour, baking soda and salt. Shape dough into 32 (1½-inch) balls. Press 1 ball in bottom and up side of each muffin cup.

3. Bake 9 to 12 minutes or until set and edges are light golden brown. Cool 1 minute; remove from pan to cooling racks. Cool completely, about 15 minutes.

4. In small bowl, beat powdered sugar, 3 tablespoons butter, food color and enough milk with electric mixer on medium speed until smooth and creamy. Stir in ¼ cup of the crushed candies. Spoon 1 rounded measuring teaspoon filling into each tart shell. Sprinkle with remaining ¼ cup crushed candies. Store in refrigerator.

1 Tartlet: Calories 130; Total Fat 4g (Saturated Fat 2.5g, Trans Fat 0g); Cholesterol 15mg; Sodium 60mg; Total Carbohydrate 21g (Dietary Fiber 0g); Protein 0g **Exchanges:** 1½ Other Carbohydrate, 1 Fat **Carbohydrate Choices:** 1½

Tinsel Time Tips

Use green food color to make green frosting, and use crushed green candies for the topping.

To keep the tarts longer, wrap tightly, label and freeze up to 6 months.

Chocolate Peppermint Tartlets

PREP TIME: **35 Minutes** • START TO FINISH: **1 Hour 25 Minutes** • **24 tartlets**

TART SHELLS

1 pouch Betty Crocker® double chocolate chunk or chocolate chunk cookie mix

3 tablespoons vegetable oil

1 tablespoon water

1 egg

½ teaspoon peppermint extract

FILLING AND TOPPING

2½ cups powdered sugar

¼ cup crushed peppermint candies (about 14)

3 tablespoons butter, softened

2 to 3 drops red food color

3 to 4 tablespoons milk

Powdered sugar

1. Heat oven to 375°F. Lightly spray 24 mini muffin cups with cooking spray. Prepare cookie dough as directed on package except use 3 tablespoons oil, 1 tablespoon water, 1 egg and the peppermint extract. Shape dough into 24 (1-inch) balls; place 1 ball in each muffin cup.

2. Bake 8 to 10 minutes or until set. Immediately make indentation in center of each cookie with end of wooden spoon to form a cup. Cool 30 minutes. Remove from pan to cooling rack; cool completely.

3. In medium bowl, beat powdered sugar, crushed candies, butter, food color and enough milk with electric mixer on medium speed until smooth and creamy. Spoon frosting into decorating bag with large star tip (#5). Pipe filling into each cookie cup. Sprinkle with powdered sugar. Store in refrigerator.

1 Tartlet: Calories 190; Total Fat 6g (Saturated Fat 2.5g, Trans Fat 0g); Cholesterol 15mg; Sodium 105mg; Total Carbohydrate 32g (Dietary Fiber 0g); Protein 1g **Exchanges:** ½ Starch, 1½ Other Carbohydrate, 1 Fat **Carbohydrate Choices:** 2

Chocolate Candy Cookie Cups

1 pouch Betty Crocker® peanut butter cookie mix

Water, vegetable oil and egg called for on cookie mix pouch

18 miniature chocolate-covered peanut, caramel and nougat candy bars (1 inch square each), unwrapped

1 container (1 lb) chocolate creamy ready-to-spread frosting

Holiday candy sprinkles, if desired

1. Heat oven to 375°F. In large bowl, stir cookie mix, water, oil and egg until soft dough forms.

2. Shape dough into 36 (1-inch) balls (about 2 teaspoons each); press into ungreased mini muffin cups. Cut each candy bar in half; press 1 candy bar piece into center of each dough-lined cup.

3. Bake 9 to 11 minutes or until edges are light golden brown. Cool completely in pans, about 30 minutes. Remove from pans to serving plate.

4. Spoon frosting into decorating bag fitted with star tip. Pipe frosting into each cookie cup. Decorate with sprinkles.

1 Cookie Cup: Calories 147; Total Fat 7g (Saturated Fat 2g, Trans Fat 1g); Cholesterol 5mg; Sodium 118mg; Total Carbohydrate 20g (Dietary Fiber 0g); Protein 1g **Exchanges:** 1½ Other Carbohydrate, 1 Fat **Carbohydrate Choices:** 1½

Cookies as Gifts

Homemade cookies are the perfect choice for a seasonal thank-you or hostess gift—and they're sure to be a hit at any holiday party.

Make a Message Platter: Look for inexpensive platters at the dollar store or in the dollar section of your discount store. Write a simple message near the edge of the platter, such as "Happy Holidays" or "Merry Christmas," in melted chocolate or with packaged cookie icing. Let it harden before arranging cookies on the platter (lined with a paper doily), leaving room for the words to show. Wrap with plastic wrap or see-through red and green plastic giftwrap and tie with a ribbon.

Create with Unusual Containers: To make giving cookies even more fun, put them in unusual containers (see Fudge-Filled Peanut Butter Cookies, page 48). Christmas stockings, festive mailing tubes or canning jars make great choices. Line with plastic wrap, waxed paper or pretty tissue paper. Provide a cushion at the bottom—so the cookies won't break—with a layer of shredded paper for gift baskets or crumpled tissue paper or a cloth napkin.

Decorate for the Occasion: Craft stores are a mecca for interesting cookie containers. Consider decorative tins (see Baked Hazelnut Truffles, page 136), Chinese take-out containers, wooden or paper boxes or decorative bags. Decorate plain containers with sprigs of plastic holly, mini candy canes or paper snowflakes instead of doilies.

Send a Cookie Envelope: Place one large cookie on a square of waxed paper the size of the cookie. Place the waxed paper on a larger decorative sheet of heavy-weight paper. (Measure the diameter of the cookie and use a square of paper that's double the size.) Fold the corners of paper to the middle of the cookie (overlapping the edges slightly); secure with a self-sticking seal. Or use CD envelopes to hold individual cookies.

Reuse/Recycle Containers: Reuse restaurant take-out containers (see Decorate-Before-You-Bake Cookies, page 104). Many restaurants use sturdy plastic containers with clear lids for take-out orders. Hand-wash, dry and keep them on hand for easy holiday cookie gift-giving.

Fill a Pretty Glass or Cup: Use a martini glass, teacup, coffee mug, etc., picked up at a garage sale or thrift shop for a fun presentation. Wrap it in red and green plastic giftwrap or tulle fabric and tie with a colorful ribbon. The container continues to be a gift long after the cookies are eaten!

Separate for Interest: Add interest and keep cookies from breaking by tightly lining up several cookies next to each other in paper baking cups and arranging several of these filled cups in a baking pan or drawer organizer or on a pretty platter.

Color in the Empty Spaces: Fill spaces between cookies arranged in flat containers with festive colorful candies, like gumdrops or nonpareils, to add interest, provide an extra treat and help keep cookies from moving and breaking.

GLUTEN-FREE

Peanut Butter Cookie Cups

PREP TIME: **55 Minutes** • START TO FINISH: **1 Hour 30 Minutes** • **5 dozen cookies**

1	box Betty Crocker® Gluten Free chocolate chip cookie mix
1	egg
½	cup butter, softened
1	teaspoon gluten-free vanilla
½	cup creamy peanut butter
60	miniature chocolate-covered peanut butter cup candies, unwrapped

1. Heat oven to 375°F. Place mini paper baking cup in each of 24 mini muffin cups.

2. In large bowl, mix cookie mix, egg, butter and vanilla with spoon. Stir in peanut butter. Shape dough into 60 (1-inch) balls. Place 1 ball in each muffin cup.

3. Bake 9 to 11 minutes or until just lightly browned. Immediately press peanut butter cup candy into center of each cookie. Cool 5 minutes before removing from pans to cooling racks; cool completely. Repeat with remaining dough.

1 Cookie: Calories 100; Total Fat 5g (Saturated Fat 2g, Trans Fat 0g); Cholesterol 10mg; Sodium 80mg; Total Carbohydrate 11g (Dietary Fiber 0g); Protein 1g **Exchanges:** ½ Starch, ½ Other Carbohydrate, 1 Fat **Carbohydrate Choices:** 1

Tinsel Time Tip

Cooking gluten free? Always read labels to make sure each recipe ingredient is gluten free. Products and ingredient sources can change.

Almond Linzer Cookies

PREP TIME: **1 Hour 15 Minutes** • START TO FINISH: **2 Hours** • **32 sandwich cookies**

1 pouch Betty Crocker sugar cookie mix

⅓ cup slivered almonds, toasted, finely chopped*

⅓ cup butter, melted

½ teaspoon almond extract

1 egg

⅔ cup seedless raspberry jam

⅓ cup dark or semisweet chocolate chips

1. Heat oven to 375°F. In large bowl, stir cookie mix and almonds. Stir in melted butter, almond extract and egg until stiff dough forms.

2. On floured surface, roll half of dough to ¼-inch thickness. Cut with 2-inch round, fluted or star cookie cutter. On ungreased cookie sheets, place cutouts 2 inches apart.

3. Bake 7 to 9 minutes or until set. Cool 5 minutes; remove from cookie sheets to cooling racks. Cool completely.

4. Meanwhile, on floured surface, roll other half of dough to ¼-inch thickness. Cut with linzer cutter with hole in center, OR cut with same 2-inch round cookie cutter and use 1-inch round cutter to cut hole out of center of each cookie. On ungreased cookie sheets, place cutouts 2 inches apart.

5. Bake 7 to 9 minutes or until set. Cool 5 minutes; remove from cookie sheets to cooling racks. Cool completely.

6. For each cookie, spread 1 teaspoon jam on bottom of 1 whole cookie; top with cutout cookie bottom side down. In small microwavable bowl, microwave chocolate chips uncovered on High about 1 minute, stirring after 30 seconds, until melted and stirred smooth. Using tip of fork or knife, drizzle chocolate in lines over cookies. Let stand 45 minutes or until chocolate is set.

To toast almonds, bake in ungreased shallow pan at 375°F for 6 to 10 minutes, stirring occasionally, until light brown.

1 Sandwich Cookie: Calories 120; Total Fat 4.5g (Saturated Fat 2g, Trans Fat 0.5g); Cholesterol 10mg; Sodium 55mg; Total Carbohydrate 18g (Dietary Fiber 0g); Protein 1g **Exchanges:** ½ Starch, ½ Other Carbohydrate, 1 Fat **Carbohydrate Choices:** 1

Tinsel Time Tips

You can sprinkle the cookies with powdered sugar instead of drizzling with chocolate.

Store the cookies between sheets of waxed paper in a tightly covered container.

Linzer Cookies

PREP TIME: **1 Hour** • START TO FINISH: **4 Hours** • **26 sandwich cookies**

¾ cup hazelnuts (filberts)

½ cup packed light brown sugar

2½ cups all-purpose flour

2 teaspoons cream of tartar

1 teaspoon baking soda

½ teaspoon salt

¼ teaspoon ground cinnamon

1 cup butter, softened

1 egg

1 teaspoon vanilla

Powdered sugar, if desired

½ cup seedless raspberry jam

1. Heat oven to 350°F. Spread hazelnuts in ungreased shallow baking pan. Bake uncovered about 6 minutes, stirring occasionally. Rub nuts in a kitchen towel to remove loose skins (some skins may not come off); cool 5 to 10 minutes. Turn off oven.

2. In food processor bowl with metal blade, place nuts and ¼ cup of the brown sugar. Cover; process with about 10 on-and-off pulses, 2 to 3 seconds each, until nuts are finely ground but not oily. In small bowl, mix flour, cream of tartar, baking soda, salt and cinnamon; set aside.

3. In large bowl, beat butter and remaining ¼ cup brown sugar with electric mixer on medium speed about 3 minutes or until smooth. Add nut mixture; beat about 1 minute or until mixed. Beat in egg and vanilla. With spoon, stir in flour mixture just until blended. Shape dough into 2 balls; flatten each into a round. Wrap separately in plastic wrap; refrigerate at least 2 hours or until firm.

4. Heat oven to 425°F. Remove 1 dough round from refrigerator. On well-floured surface, roll dough with floured rolling pin until about ⅛ inch thick. Cut with 2½-inch cookie cutter in desired shape. On ungreased cookie sheets, place cutouts about 1 inch apart.

5. Roll and cut other half of dough. Using a 1-inch square or round cutter, cut out the center of half of the cookies. Reroll dough centers and cut out more cookies.

6. Bake 4 to 5 minutes or until edges are light golden brown. Remove from cookie sheets to cooling racks. Cool 10 minutes. Lightly sprinkle powdered sugar over cookies with center cutouts. For each sandwich cookie, spread about 1 teaspoon raspberry jam over bottom of 1 whole cookie; top with cutout cookie, bottom side down. Cool completely, about 1 hour.

1 Sandwich Cookie: Calories 170; Total Fat 9g (Saturated Fat 4.5g, Trans Fat 0g); Cholesterol 25mg; Sodium 150mg; Total Carbohydrate 18g (Dietary Fiber 0g); Protein 2g **Exchanges:** ½ Starch, ½ Other Carbohydrate, 2 Fat **Carbohydrate Choices:** 1

Tinsel Time Tip

Drizzle these cookies with chocolate instead of sprinkling with powdered sugar. For a pop of color, decorate with a variety of sugars or candy sprinkles.

Lemon Snowdrops

PREP TIME: 1 Hour 10 Minutes • **START TO FINISH: 1 Hour 10 Minutes** • **2 dozen sandwich cookies**

COOKIES

1	cup butter, softened
½	cup powdered sugar
1	teaspoon lemon extract
2	cups all-purpose flour
¼	teaspoon salt
	Granulated sugar
	Powdered sugar

FILLING

¼	cup granulated sugar
2¼	teaspoons cornstarch
¼	cup water
1	tablespoon butter
1	teaspoon grated lemon peel
4½	teaspoons lemon juice
	Yellow food color, if desired

1. Heat oven to 400°F. In large bowl, beat 1 cup butter, ½ cup powdered sugar and the lemon extract with electric mixer on medium speed until well blended. Stir in flour and salt until dough forms. (If dough is soft, cover and refrigerate 1 to 2 hours or until firm enough to shape.)

2. Shape dough into 48 (1-inch) balls. On ungreased cookie sheets, place balls about 1 inch apart. Press bottom of glass into dough, pressing slightly. Then dip glass into granulated sugar; press on shaped dough until ¼ inch thick.

3. Bake 8 to 10 minutes or until edges are light brown. Immediately remove from cookie sheets to cooling racks. Cool completely, about 15 minutes.

4. In 1-quart saucepan, mix ¼ cup granulated sugar and the cornstarch. Stir in remaining filling ingredients. Cook over medium heat, stirring constantly, until mixture thickens and boils. Boil and stir 1 minute. Cool completely, about 15 minutes.

5. For each sandwich cookie, spread filling on bottom of 1 cookie; top with second cookie, bottom side down. Sprinkle with powdered sugar.

1 Sandwich Cookie: Calories 130; Total Fat 8g (Saturated Fat 5g, Trans Fat 0g); Cholesterol 20mg; Sodium 85mg; Total Carbohydrate 14g (Dietary Fiber 0g); Protein 1g **Exchanges:** ½ Starch, ½ Other Carbohydrate, 1½ Fat **Carbohydrate Choices:** 1

Orange Snowdrops: Use orange extract, orange peel and orange juice for the lemon extract, peel and juice.

Tinsel Time Tip

A holiday teacup filled with these cookies and wrapped tea bags makes a treasured gift.

Chocolate Chip Sandwich Cookies

PREP TIME: **15 Minutes** • START TO FINISH: **1 Hour** • **22 sandwich cookies**

COOKIES

1	box Betty Crocker Gluten Free chocolate chip cookie mix
½	cup butter, softened
1	teaspoon gluten-free vanilla
1	egg, beaten
¼	cup granulated sugar

FILLING

1	cup semisweet chocolate chips
½	cup creamy peanut butter
⅓	cup whipping cream
⅔	cup powdered sugar

1. Heat oven to 350°F. In medium bowl, stir cookie mix, butter, vanilla and egg until soft dough forms (dough will be crumbly).

2. In small bowl, place granulated sugar. Shape dough into 44 (1-inch) balls. Roll in sugar. On ungreased cookie sheets, place balls 2 inches apart. With smooth-bottomed glass, flatten each ball to about ¼-inch thickness.

3. Bake 8 to 10 minutes or until edges are lightly browned. Remove from cookie sheets to cooling racks. Cool completely, about 30 minutes.

4. In medium bowl, place chocolate chips and peanut butter. In small microwavable bowl, microwave whipping cream on High 30 to 60 seconds. Pour cream over chips and peanut butter; stir until chips are melted. Stir in powdered sugar until smooth.

5. For each sandwich cookie, spread 1 tablespoon filling on bottom of 1 cookie; top with second cookie, bottom side down. Let stand until set.

1 Sandwich Cookie: Calories 260; Total Fat 13g (Saturated Fat 6g, Trans Fat 0g); Cholesterol 25mg; Sodium 180mg; Total Carbohydrate 33g (Dietary Fiber 0g); Protein 3g **Exchanges:** ½ Starch, 1½ Other Carbohydrate, 2½ Fat **Carbohydrate Choices:** 2

Tinsel Time Tips

Roll the edges of the cookies in finely chopped peanuts, if you like.

Cooking gluten free? Always read labels to make sure each recipe ingredient is gluten free. Products and ingredient sources can change.

Hazelnut–Peanut Butter Sandwich Cookies

PREP TIME: **30 minutes** • START TO FINISH: **1 Hour 20 Minutes** • **2½ dozen sandwich cookies**

COOKIES

1	pouch Betty Crocker peanut butter cookie mix
⅓	cup butter, softened
1	egg

FILLING

1	cup hazelnut spread with cocoa
¼	cup powdered sugar

1. Heat oven to 375°F. In large bowl, stir cookie ingredients until stiff dough forms. Shape dough into 60 (1-inch) balls. On ungreased cookie sheets, place balls about 2 inches apart.

2. Bake 7 to 9 minutes or until set. Cool 2 minutes; remove from cookie sheets to cooling racks. Cool completely, about 30 minutes.

3. In small bowl, mix filling ingredients. Spoon filling into decorating bag fitted with ⅜-inch star tip. For each sandwich cookie, pipe filling around outer edge of bottom of 1 cookie; top with second cookie, bottom side down. Do not press together.

1 Sandwich Cookie: Calories 110; Total Fat 5g (Saturated Fat 2g, Trans Fat 0g); Cholesterol 10mg; Sodium 105mg; Total Carbohydrate 14g (Dietary Fiber 0g); Protein 1g **Exchanges:** ½ Starch, ½ Other Carbohydrate, 1 Fat **Carbohydrate Choices:** 1

Tinsel Time Tip

For an extra-special look, sprinkle your cookies with powdered sugar or baking cocoa.

Gingersnap Sandwich Cookies

PREP TIME: **1 Hour 10 Minutes**   •   START TO FINISH: **3 Hours 40 Minutes**   •   **34 sandwich cookies**

COOKIES

- ½   cup butter, softened
- ¼   cup granulated sugar
- ¼   cup packed brown sugar
- ½   cup molasses
- ¼   cup cold water
- 2½ cups all-purpose flour
- 2   teaspoons ground ginger
- 2   teaspoons ground cinnamon
- 1   teaspoon baking soda
- ½   teaspoon ground cloves
- ¼   teaspoon salt

FROSTING

- 3   cups powdered sugar
- ½   cup butter, softened
- 2   teaspoons grated lemon peel
- 3   to 4 teaspoons lemon juice
- 3   to 4 teaspoons milk
- Additional grated lemon peel, if desired

1. In large bowl, beat ½ cup butter and the sugars with electric mixer on medium speed until light and fluffy. Beat in molasses and water until blended (mixture may look curdled). On low speed, beat in flour, ginger, cinnamon, baking soda, cloves and salt. Divide dough in half; wrap each half in plastic wrap. Refrigerate about 2 hours or until chilled.

2. Heat oven to 350°F. Line cookie sheets with cooking parchment paper. On well-floured surface, roll half of dough at a time to ⅛-inch thickness (keep remaining dough refrigerated). Cut with 2-inch round cookie cutter. Using large end of a piping tip or ½-inch round canapé cutter, cut a hole in center of half of the cutouts. Carefully transfer to cookie sheets, placing ½ inch apart. Reroll scraps.

3. Bake 9 to 12 minutes or until set in center. Cool 2 minutes; remove from cookie sheets to cooling racks. Cool completely, about 30 minutes.

4. In large bowl, beat frosting ingredients on medium speed until light and fluffy. For each sandwich cookie, spread about 1 heaping teaspoon frosting on bottom of 1 whole cookie; top with cutout cookie, bottom side down. Sprinkle additional grated lemon peel on frosting in center.

1 Sandwich Cookie: Calories 150; Total Fat 6g (Saturated Fat 3.5g, Trans Fat 0g); Cholesterol 15mg; Sodium 95mg; Total Carbohydrate 25g (Dietary Fiber 0g); Protein 1g **Exchanges:** ½ Starch, 1 Other Carbohydrate, 1 Fat **Carbohydrate Choices:** 1½

Tinsel Time Tips

For faster chilling time, roll half of the dough at a time between two sheets of cooking parchment paper. Refrigerate about 15 minutes.

For the best flavor, be sure to use spices that are no older than 6 months.

Fudge-Filled
Peanut Butter Cookies

PREP TIME: **1 Hour 10 Minutes** • START TO FINISH: **2 Hours 10 Minutes** • **2 dozen sandwich cookies**

¾   cup creamy peanut butter

½   cup shortening

½   cup granulated sugar

½   cup packed brown sugar

1   egg

1⅓ cups all-purpose flour

1   teaspoon baking powder

½   teaspoon baking soda

1   cup semisweet chocolate
    chips

1. Heat oven to 375°F. In large bowl, beat ½ cup of the peanut butter, the shortening, and the sugars with electric mixer on medium speed until fluffy. Beat in egg until smooth. Beat in flour, baking powder and baking soda.

2. Shape dough into 48 (1-inch) balls. On ungreased cookie sheets, place balls 1 inch apart. Flatten balls to ¼-inch thickness by pressing with fork in a crisscross pattern.

3. Bake 4 to 8 minutes or until bottoms are golden brown. Remove from cookie sheets to cooling racks. Cool completely, about 30 minutes.

4. In small microwavable bowl, microwave chocolate chips uncovered on High about 1 minute or until softened; stir until smooth. Stir remaining ¼ cup peanut butter into chocolate until smooth. Cool to room temperature or until thickened.

5. For each sandwich cookie, spread 1 teaspoon chocolate mixture on bottom of 1 cookie; top with second cookie, bottom side down. Let stand about 1 hour or until chocolate is firm.

1 Sandwich Cookie: Calories 190; Total Fat 11g (Saturated Fat 3g, Trans Fat 1g); Cholesterol 10mg; Sodium 90mg; Total Carbohydrate 20g (Dietary Fiber 1g); Protein 3g **Exchanges:** 1 Starch, ½ Other Carbohydrate, 2 Fat **Carbohydrate Choices:** 1

Whoopie Pies

PREP TIME: **45 Minutes** • START TO FINISH: **1 Hour 25 Minutes** • **1½ dozen whoopie pies**

COOKIES

1	cup granulated sugar
½	cup butter, softened
½	cup buttermilk
2	teaspoons vanilla
1	egg
2	oz unsweetened baking chocolate, melted, cooled
1¾	cups all-purpose flour
½	teaspoon baking soda
½	teaspoon salt

FILLING

3	cups powdered sugar
1	jar (7 oz) marshmallow creme
¾	cup butter, softened
6	to 7 teaspoons milk

DECORATION

Crushed peppermint candies or candy canes

1. Heat oven to 400°F. Grease cookie sheet with shortening or cooking spray, or line with cooking parchment paper.

2. In large bowl, beat granulated sugar, ½ cup butter, the buttermilk, vanilla, egg and chocolate with electric mixer on medium speed, or mix with spoon, until well blended. Stir in flour, baking soda and salt. On cookie sheets, drop dough by rounded tablespoonfuls about 2 inches apart.

3. Bake 8 to 10 minutes or until almost no indentation remains when touched in center. Immediately remove from cookie sheets to cooling racks. Cool completely, about 30 minutes.

4. In large bowl, beat all filling ingredients on medium speed about 2 minutes or until light and fluffy. For each whoopie pie, spread scant 3 tablespoons filling on bottom of 1 cookie; top with second cookie, bottom side down. Sprinkle edges of filling with crushed candies. Store in tightly covered container.

1 Whoopie Pie: Calories 350; Total Fat 15g (Saturated Fat 9g, Trans Fat 0.5g); Cholesterol 45mg; Sodium 210mg; Total Carbohydrate 50g (Dietary Fiber 1g); Protein 2g **Exchanges:** 1 Starch, 2½ Other Carbohydrate, 3 Fat **Carbohydrate Choices:** 3

Pink Peppermint Whoopie Pies: Add 6 drops red food color to filling ingredients. Once cookies are assembled, sprinkle edges of filling with crushed peppermint candies or candy canes.

Chocolate Chip Whoopie Pies: Fold ½ cup miniature semisweet chocolate chips into the filling.

Toffee Whoopie Pies: Fold ½ cup chocolate-covered toffee bits into the filling.

Chocolate-Mallow Cookie Pies

PREP TIME: **50 Minutes** • START TO FINISH: **1 Hour 10 Minutes** • **1½ dozen cookie pies**

COOKIES

1   pouch Betty Crocker sugar cookie mix

⅓   cup unsweetened baking cocoa

2   tablespoons all-purpose flour

⅓   cup sour cream

¼   cup butter, softened

1   teaspoon vanilla

1   egg

FILLING

⅔   cup marshmallow creme

⅓   cup butter, softened

½   teaspoon vanilla

⅔   cup powdered sugar

TOPPING

1   tablespoon powdered sugar

⅛   teaspoon unsweetened baking cocoa

1. Heat oven to 350°F. In large bowl, stir cookie mix, ⅓ cup cocoa and the flour. Add sour cream, ¼ cup butter, 1 teaspoon vanilla and the egg; stir until stiff dough forms. Shape dough into 36 (1-inch) balls. On ungreased cookie sheets, place balls 2 inches apart. Press each ball to flatten slightly.

2. Bake 8 to 9 minutes or until set (do not overbake). Cool 2 minutes; remove from cookie sheets to cooling racks. Cool completely, about 15 minutes.

3. In small bowl, beat filling ingredients with electric mixer until light and fluffy. For each cookie pie, spread about 2 teaspoons filling on bottom of 1 cooled cookie. Top with second cookie bottom side down; gently press cookies together.

4. In small bowl, stir together topping ingredients. Sprinkle over tops of cookie pies. Store between sheets of waxed paper in tightly covered container.

1 Cookie Pie: Calories 220; Total Fat 10g (Saturated Fat 5g, Trans Fat 1.5g); Cholesterol 30mg; Sodium 130mg; Total Carbohydrate 31g (Dietary Fiber 0g); Protein 2g **Exchanges:** 1 Starch, 1 Other Carbohydrate, 2 Fat **Carbohydrate Choices:** 2

Tinsel Time Tip

To easily scoop marshmallow creme out of the jar, use a rubber spatula lightly sprayed with cooking spray.

Mini Whoopie Pies

PREP TIME: **2 Hours** • START TO FINISH: **2 Hours** • **50 whoopie pies**

COOKIES

2	tablespoons butter, softened
½	cup granulated sugar
1½	cups Original Bisquick® mix
1	egg
1	teaspoon vanilla
	Red food color

FILLING

4	oz (half of 8-oz package) cream cheese, softened
¼	cup butter, softened
½	teaspoon vanilla
1¼	cups powdered sugar

1. Heat oven to 350°F. Line large cookie sheets with cooking parchment paper.

2. In medium bowl, beat 2 tablespoons butter and the granulated sugar with electric mixer on low speed until well blended and sandy in texture. Add Bisquick mix, egg and vanilla. Beat on medium speed 2 minutes, scraping bowl occasionally, until smooth.

3. Stir food color into batter as desired to create bright red color. Stir until well blended. Spoon batter into resealable food-storage plastic bag. Cut ¼ inch off corner of bag. Onto cookie sheets, squeeze bag of batter gently to make about 100 (½-inch) rounds of dough (about ¼ teaspoon each), about 1 inch apart.

4. Bake 3 to 5 minutes or until tops spring back when lightly touched. Cool 2 minutes; gently remove from cookie sheets to cooling racks. Cool completely, about 20 minutes.

5. In medium bowl, beat cream cheese, ¼ cup butter and ½ teaspoon vanilla with electric mixer on low speed until well mixed. Gradually add powdered sugar, beating on low speed until incorporated. Increase speed to medium; beat about 1 minute or until smooth.

6. For each whoopie pie, spread about ½ teaspoon filling on bottom of 1 cookie; top with second cookie bottom side down. Store loosely covered in refrigerator.

1 Whoopie Pie: Calories 60; Total Fat 2.5g (Saturated Fat 1.5g, Trans Fat 0g); Cholesterol 10mg; Sodium 70mg; Total Carbohydrate 8g (Dietary Fiber 0g); Protein 0g **Exchanges:** ½ Other Carbohydrate, ½ Fat **Carbohydrate Choices:** ½

Tinsel Time Tips

For a brighter pop of color, use gel food color rather than liquid.

Save time in the kitchen by making these bite-size whoopie pies a bit bigger. Use about ½ teaspoon dough per cookie. Bake 6 to 7 minutes.

chapter
two

Ready to Roll

Snowman "Star" Cutouts

PREP TIME: **1 Hour 30 Minutes** • START TO FINISH: **1 Hour 30 Minutes** • **2 dozen cookies**

1   pouch Betty Crocker sugar cookie mix

2   tablespoons all-purpose flour

⅓   cup butter, softened

1   egg

1   tube (4.25 oz) black decorating icing

1   container (12 oz) whipped fluffy white ready-to-spread frosting

Coarse white decorating sugar

Assorted candies

1. Heat oven to 375°F. In medium bowl, stir cookie mix, flour, butter and egg until soft dough forms.

2. On lightly floured surface, roll dough to ⅛-inch thickness. Cut with star-shaped cookie cutter. On ungreased cookie sheets, place cutouts 1 inch apart.

3. Bake 7 to 9 minutes or until edges are light golden brown. Cool 1 minute; remove from cookie sheets to cooling racks. Cool completely, about 15 minutes.

4. Frost and decorate 1 cookie at a time. Pipe black icing on tip of star for hat. Frost remaining star with white frosting. Sprinkle with coarse sugar. Attach candies for buttons and face.

1 Frosted Cookie (Undecorated): Calories 170; Total Fat 8g (Saturated Fat 3g, Trans Fat 1.5g); Cholesterol 15mg; Sodium 95mg; Total Carbohydrate 25g (Dietary Fiber 0g); Protein 1g **Exchanges:** ½ Starch, 1 Other Carbohydrate, 1½ Fat **Carbohydrate Choices:** 1½

Tinsel Time Tip

You can freeze baked cookies for up to 2 months.

GLUTEN-FREE

Ultimate Cutout Cookies

PREP TIME: **55 Minutes** • START TO FINISH: **55 Minutes** • **About 1½ dozen cookies**

½ cup powdered sugar

1 package (3 oz) cream cheese, softened

⅓ cup butter, softened

3 tablespoons shortening

1 teaspoon gluten-free vanilla

1 egg yolk

1½ cups Bisquick® Gluten Free mix

Additional powdered sugar for work surface

1 container (1 lb) vanilla creamy ready-to-spread frosting, if desired

1. Heat oven to 375°F. Lightly grease cookie sheets with shortening or cooking spray. In large bowl, stir ½ cup powdered sugar, cream cheese, butter, shortening, vanilla and egg yolk with spoon until well blended. Stir in Bisquick mix until dough forms.

2. On work surface sprinkled with additional powdered sugar, roll half of dough at a time to ¼-inch thickness. Cut with cookie cutters. Use metal spatula to transfer cookie cutouts to cookie sheets, placing cutouts about 1 inch apart.

3. Bake 6 to 8 minutes or until edges are light golden brown. Cool 2 minutes; carefully remove from cookie sheets to cooling racks. Cool completely, about 15 minutes. Frost cookies.

1 Cookie: Calories 120; Total Fat 8g (Saturated Fat 3.5g, Trans Fat 0.5g); Cholesterol 25mg; Sodium 140mg; Total Carbohydrate 11g (Dietary Fiber 0g); Protein 1g **Exchanges:** ½ Starch, 1½ Fat **Carbohydrate Choices:** 1

Tinsel Time Tips

Cooking gluten free? Always read labels to make sure each recipe ingredient is gluten free. Products and ingredient sources can change.

To make ahead, keep unfrosted baked cookies in the freezer for up to 2 months, ready for the kids to frost and decorate.

Santa Bell Cookies

PREP TIME: **45 Minutes** • START TO FINISH: **2 Hours 20 Minutes** • **1 dozen cookies**

COOKIES

- 1 pouch Betty Crocker sugar cookie mix
- ½ cup butter, softened
- 1 tablespoon all-purpose flour
- 1 egg
- ½ teaspoon almond extract

FROSTING AND DECORATIONS

- 1 pouch (7 oz) white decorating icing
- ½ cup flaked coconut
- 2 tablespoons red decorating icing (from 7-oz pouch)
- 2 tablespoons coarse red sparkling sugar
- 24 brown candy-coated milk chocolate candies
- 12 red cinnamon candies

1. In large bowl, stir cookie mix, butter, flour, egg and almond extract until soft dough forms. Shape dough into ball; flatten slightly. Wrap in plastic wrap; refrigerate 1 hour.

2. Heat oven to 375°F. Unwrap dough. On floured surface, roll dough to ¼-inch thickness. Cut with floured 4¾-inch bell-shaped cookie cutter. On ungreased cookie sheets, place cutouts 2 inches apart. Bake 10 to 12 minutes or until edges are lightly browned. Cool 2 minutes; remove from cookie sheets to cooling racks. Cool completely, about 30 minutes.

3. For each cookie, spread or pipe white icing onto bottom of bell for beard and mustache and onto top of bell for hat pom-pom; sprinkle with coconut. Pipe red icing under pom-pom for hat; sprinkle with red sugar. Use white icing to attach milk chocolate candies for eyes and cinnamon candies for nose. Pipe red icing for mouth and white icing for eyebrows. Let stand until set.

1 Cookie: Calories 370; Total Fat 16g (Saturated Fat 7g, Trans Fat 0g); Cholesterol 0mg; Sodium 230mg; Total Carbohydrate 55g (Dietary Fiber 0g); Protein 2g **Exchanges:** ½ Starch, 3 Other Carbohydrate, 3 Fat **Carbohydrate Choices:** 3½

Sugar Cookie Presents

PREP TIME: **45 Minutes** • START TO FINISH: **2 Hours 20 Minutes** • **1½ dozen cookies**

COOKIES

- 1 pouch Betty Crocker sugar cookie mix
- ⅓ cup butter, softened
- 2 tablespoons all-purpose flour
- 1 egg

FROSTING AND DECORATIONS

- 1 cup fluffy white whipped ready-to-spread frosting (from 12-oz container)
- ½ teaspoon yellow paste food color
- ¼ teaspoon green paste food color
- 4 rolls strawberry fruit-flavored snacks in 3-foot rolls (from 4.5-oz box)
- 2 tablespoons white nonpareils

1. In large bowl, stir cookie mix, butter, flour and egg until dough forms. Shape dough into ball; flatten slightly. Wrap in plastic wrap; refrigerate 1 hour.

2. Heat oven to 375°F. Unwrap dough; on floured surface, roll dough to ¼-inch thickness. Cut with floured 3-inch present-shaped cookie cutter. On ungreased cookie sheets, place cutouts 2 inches apart. Bake 9 to 11 minutes or until lightly browned. Cool 2 minutes; remove from cookie sheets to cooling racks. Cool completely, about 30 minutes.

3. In small bowl, mix frosting and food colors until well blended. Frost cookies. Cut and shape fruit snacks to look like ribbons and bows; place on cookies. Sprinkle with nonpareils. Let stand until set.

1 Cookie: Calories 230; Total Fat 9g (Saturated Fat 4g, Trans Fat 0g); Cholesterol 0mg; Sodium 120mg; Total Carbohydrate 34g (Dietary Fiber 0g); Protein 2g **Exchanges:** ½ Starch, 2 Other Carbohydrate, 1½ Fat **Carbohydrate Choices:** 2½

Snowflake Mittens

PREP TIME: **1 Hour** • START TO FINISH: **1 Hour 45 Minutes** • **21 cookies**

COOKIES

1	pouch Betty Crocker sugar cookie mix
1	tablespoon all-purpose flour
⅓	cup butter, softened
1	egg
1	tablespoon grated lemon peel

FROSTING AND DECORATIONS

1	container (1 lb) creamy white ready-to-spread frosting
3	drops blue food color
1	can (6.4 oz) white decorating icing
	White snowflake-shaped candy sprinkles or other white candy sprinkles, if desired

1. Heat oven to 375°F. In large bowl, stir cookie mix, flour, butter, egg and lemon peel until dough forms; shape into ball. Divide dough in half; shape into 2 rounds. Wrap 1 round in plastic wrap.

2. On floured surface, roll unwrapped round to ¼-inch thickness. Cut with floured 3½-inch mitten-shaped cookie cutter. On ungreased cookie sheets, place cutouts 1 inch apart. Repeat with second round. Reroll the scraps and cut out additional cookies.

3. Bake 8 to 10 minutes or until edges are lightly browned. Cool 1 minute; remove from cookie sheets to cooling racks. Cool completely, about 30 minutes.

4. Using ½ cup of the creamy white frosting, frost cuffs of mittens. Stir food color into remaining white frosting. Frost remaining portion of mittens with blue frosting. With decorating icing and small round tip, pipe small snowflake on each mitten. With star tip, decorate cuffs of mittens with decorating icing, if desired. Decorate with candy sprinkles. Let stand until set.

1 Cookie: Calories 130; Total Fat 5g (Saturated Fat 2.5g, Trans Fat 1g); Cholesterol 20mg; Sodium 90mg; Total Carbohydrate 18g (Dietary Fiber 0g); Protein 1g **Exchanges:** ½ Starch, ½ Other Carbohydrate, 1 Fat **Carbohydrate Choices:** 1

Tinsel Time Tips

Spoon some of the blue frosting into a small resealable food-storage plastic bag, and cut off a tiny corner of the bag. Pipe each child's name across the cuff of a mitten. Just for fun, attach rick-rack with a dab of frosting to connect two cookies as a cute gift.

Bake the cookies a day ahead and store them in an airtight container. Get the frosting and decorating items ready, and let the kids help decorate.

Porcelain Cookies

PREP TIME: **1 Hour 30 Minutes** • START TO FINISH: **3 Hours 30 Minutes** • **About 32 cookies**

COOKIES

- ¾ cup butter, softened
- ¾ cup granulated sugar
- 1 egg
- 1 tablespoon finely grated lemon peel
- 2 tablespoons lemon juice
- 2½ cups all-purpose flour
- 1 teaspoon baking soda
- ¼ teaspoon salt

ICING

- 3 cups powdered sugar
- 2 tablespoons meringue powder
- 5 teaspoons lemon juice
- 4 to 5 tablespoons water

DECORATIONS

- Colored sugars
- Colored candy sprinkles

Tinsel Time Tip

These cookies store well. Once the icings are set (including the decorations), place the cookies in a firm tin or plastic container and freeze. They can be kept up to 2 months.

1. In large bowl, beat butter and granulated sugar with electric mixer on medium speed until creamy. On low speed, beat in egg, lemon peel and 2 tablespoons lemon juice. Stir in flour, baking soda and salt until well blended. Divide dough into 4 parts; flatten each into ½-inch-thick round. Wrap each in waxed paper or plastic wrap. Refrigerate 30 minutes.

2. Heat oven to 350°F. Remove 1 round of dough at a time from refrigerator. Between sheets of floured waxed paper or plastic wrap, roll dough to ¼- to ⅜-inch thickness. Cut with 3-inch cookie cutters. On ungreased cookie sheets, place cutouts 1 inch apart.

3. Bake 10 to 12 minutes or just until edges are golden. Cool on cookie sheets about 1 minute before removing to cooling rack. To make cookies for hanging, using toothpick or end of plastic straw, carefully poke a hole in the top of each cookie while cookies are still hot. Cool 10 to 15 minutes before adding icing.

4. In medium bowl, stir powdered sugar and meringue powder. Stir in 5 teaspoons lemon juice and enough of the 4 to 5 tablespoons water to make a thin icing. Transfer ½ cup of the icing into small bowl; set aside. Using flexible pastry brush, paint cookies to the edges with icing. Place on cooling rack to dry completely, about 30 minutes.

5. Beat reserved icing with electric mixer on high speed 5 to 7 minutes or until peaks form. Place in small resealable food-storage plastic bag; cut small tip off 1 corner. Squeeze icing onto glazed cookies. Before icing dries, sprinkle with decorations; tap off excess. Dry completely on cooling rack. Thread cookies with ribbon for hanging.

1 Iced Cookie (Undecorated): Calories 150; Total Fat 4.5g (Saturated Fat 3g, Trans Fat 0g); Cholesterol 20mg; Sodium 100mg; Total Carbohydrate 25g (Dietary Fiber 0g); Protein 2g **Exchanges:** ½ Starch, 1 Other Carbohydrate, 1 Fat **Carbohydrate Choices:** 1½

Holiday Cutouts

PREP TIME: **1 Hour** • START TO FINISH: **4 Hours 10 Minutes** • **5 dozen cookies**

COOKIES

1½	cups powdered sugar
1	cup butter, softened
1	teaspoon vanilla
½	teaspoon almond extract
1	egg
2½	cups all-purpose flour
1	teaspoon baking soda
1	teaspoon cream of tartar

FROSTING

2	cups powdered sugar
½	teaspoon vanilla
2	tablespoons milk or half-and-half
	Food color, if desired

DECORATIONS

Colored sugars, candy sprinkles and nonpareils, if desired

1. In large bowl, mix 1½ cups powdered sugar, the butter, 1 teaspoon vanilla, the almond extract and egg until well blended. Stir in flour, baking soda and cream of tartar. Cover and refrigerate at least 3 hours.

2. Heat oven to 375°F. Divide dough in half. On lightly floured, cloth-covered surface, roll each half of dough to ³⁄₁₆-inch thickness. Cut into assorted shapes with cookie cutters, or cut around patterns traced from storybook illustrations. If cookies are to be hung as decorations, make a hole in each ¼ inch from top using end of plastic straw. On ungreased cookie sheets, place cutouts 1 inch apart.

3. Bake 7 to 8 minutes or until light brown. Remove from cookie sheets to cooling racks. Cool completely, about 30 minutes.

4. In medium bowl, beat frosting ingredients until smooth and spreadable. Tint with food color if desired. Frost and decorate cookies as desired with frosting and colored sugars.

1 Cookie: Calories 80; Total Fat 3.5g (Saturated Fat 2g, Trans Fat 0g); Cholesterol 10mg; Sodium 45mg; Total Carbohydrate 11g (Dietary Fiber 0g); Protein 0g **Exchanges:** 1 Other Carbohydrate, ½ Fat **Carbohydrate Choices:** 1

Tinsel Time Tips

For melt-in-your-mouth treats, be sure to mix cookies just enough—but not too much. Too much mixing can result in tough cookies.

Skip the homemade frosting and use part of a container of ready-to-spread frosting instead. The frosting layer will be a bit thicker this way, but it will be equally delicious!

Christmas Cookie Packages

PREP TIME: **2 Hours 10 Minutes** • START TO FINISH: **3 Hours 40 Minutes** • **About 5 dozen cookies**

COOKIES

1½	cups powdered sugar
1	cup butter, softened
1	teaspoon vanilla
½	teaspoon almond extract
1	egg
2½	cups all-purpose flour
1	teaspoon baking soda
1	teaspoon cream of tartar

FROSTING AND DECORATIONS

Decorating icings (any color from 4.25-oz tubes)

Snowflake or star candy sprinkles, if desired

Edible glitter, if desired

1. In large bowl, mix powdered sugar, butter, vanilla, almond extract and egg with spoon. Stir in flour, baking soda and cream of tartar. Cover; refrigerate about 2 hours or until firm.

2. Heat oven to 375°F. Lightly grease cookie sheets with shortening or cooking spray. Divide dough in half. On lightly floured surface, roll half of dough at a time to ¼-inch thickness. Cut into 2-inch squares. On cookie sheets, place squares 1 inch apart.

3. Bake 7 to 8 minutes or until edges are light brown. Remove from cookie sheets to cooling racks. Cool completely, about 30 minutes.

4. Decorate tops of each package with icings to form ribbon and bow. Arrange with candies and sprinkle with glitter.

1 Cookie: Calories 100; Total Fat 4.5g (Saturated Fat 2.5g, Trans Fat 0g); Cholesterol 10mg; Sodium 45mg; Total Carbohydrate 14g (Dietary Fiber 0g); Protein 0g **Exchanges:** 1 Other Carbohydrate, 1 Fat **Carbohydrate Choices:** 1

Tinsel Time Tip

If you forget to remove your cookies from the cookie sheets in time and they seem to stick, just pop the whole sheet back in the hot oven for a minute or two. The heat should soften the cookies slightly, making the cookies easier to remove.

Easy Decorating Tips

Before Baking Cookies

Add sparkle to festive treats, like Holiday Surprise Sugar Cookies (page 14), with decorating sugars. Press balls of sugar cookie dough with a greased and sugared glass bottom. Using a very small spoon, add red sugar to cookies in a spiral design to look like peppermint candies.

After Baking Cookies

Dip cookies in melted chocolate.
To melt chocolate for dipping, heat 1 teaspoon shortening with 3 ounces bittersweet, semisweet or white chocolate over low heat, stirring frequently, until chocolate is melted and smooth. Or place the chocolate in a microwavable container and microwave on High until melted and smooth, stirring every 10 to 15 seconds.

Drizzle melted chocolate over cookies.
Melt white baking chips or semisweet chocolate chips as directed above, then pour into a resealable food-storage plastic bag. Snip off a tiny corner of the bag, and squeeze the chocolate over the cookies, such as for Pecan-Shortbread Trees (page 120).

Drizzle glaze over cookies.
Place ready-to-spread frosting in a microwavable container and microwave on High until melted, stirring every 20 to 30 seconds. Spoon frosting into a resealable food-storage plastic bag. Snip off a tiny corner of the bag, and squeeze the frosting over the cookies. Sprinkle glazed cookies, such as Merry Molasses Cookies (page 92), with unsweetened baking cocoa, using a stencil. Use ready-made seasonally inspired stencils, or craft your own using miniature cookie cutters, taping over open areas to use just the outline. Place the stencil on the cookie.

Let candies star on cookies.
Press milk or dark chocolate candies into cookies immediately after baking.

Dazzle with gels.
Squeeze decorating gels over unfrosted or frosted cookies, like Festive Peanut Butter Blossom Cookies (page 142), in simple designs.

Embellish cookies with candies.
Frost cookies resembling cute Christmas favorites such as reindeer, trees, stars and Santas. It's fun to embellish cookies like the Peanut Butter Reindeer Cookies (page 140) with frosting, then decorate with candies to add the eyes and nose.

Holiday Cookie Ornaments

PREP TIME: **1 Hour 15 Minutes** • START TO FINISH: **2 Hours 15 Minutes** • **About 3 dozen cookies**

1   pouch Betty Crocker sugar
     cookie mix

⅓   cup butter, melted

2   tablespoons all-purpose flour

1   egg

36   small candy canes

2   containers (1 lb each) creamy
     white or vanilla creamy
     ready-to-spread frosting

     Assorted decorations, as
     desired

1. Heat oven to 375°F. Line cookie sheets with cooking parchment paper. In medium bowl, stir cookie mix, butter, flour and egg until soft dough forms.

2. On floured surface, roll dough to ⅛-inch thickness. Cut with 3- to 3½-inch cookie cutters. On cookie sheets, place cutouts 1 inch apart.

3. Bake 5 minutes. Meanwhile, break off top of each candy cane to create loop for hanging cookies. Remove cookies from oven; press 1 candy piece on top of each cookie to make a loop. Bake 1 to 2 minutes longer or until edges are set. Cool on cookie sheets 2 minutes. Remove from cookie sheets to cooling rack. Cool completely, about 20 minutes.

4. Line cookie sheet with cooking parchment paper. Place 1 container of frosting at a time in 2-cup glass measuring cup. Microwave on High 45 to 60 seconds, stirring every 15 seconds, until melted. Dip each cookie in frosting, allowing excess to drip off. Place cookies on parchment paper. Decorate as desired. Let stand about 1 hour or until frosting is set.

1 Cookie: Calories 200; Total Fat 9g (Saturated Fat 3.5g, Trans Fat 2.5g); Cholesterol 10mg; Sodium 110mg; Total Carbohydrate 29g (Dietary Fiber 0g); Protein 0g **Exchanges:** 2 Other Carbohydrate, 2 Fat **Carbohydrate Choices:** 2

Tinsel Time Tip

To evenly break candy canes, cut them with scissors while they're still in the wrapper, then unwrap and use.

Chocolate Chip Reindeer Cookies

PREP TIME: **1 Hour 15 Minutes** • START TO FINISH: **5 Hours 5 Minutes** • **16 cookies**

1   pouch Betty Crocker® chocolate chip cookie mix

1   tablespoon all-purpose flour

½   cup butter, softened

1   egg

2   pouches (7 oz each) chocolate decorating icing

32   candy eyes

16   small round chocolate-covered creamy mints

1   pouch (7 oz) white decorating icing

1. In large bowl, beat cookie mix, flour, butter and egg with electric mixer on low speed just until blended. Shape into ball. Flatten dough to ½-inch thickness; wrap in plastic wrap. Refrigerate 3 hours or until very firm.

2. Heat oven to 350°F. Unwrap dough; on well-floured surface, roll dough to ¼-inch thickness. Cut with floured 3½-inch gingerbread boy cookie cutter. On ungreased cookie sheets, place cutouts 2 inches apart. Refrigerate on cookie sheets 10 minutes.

3. Bake 9 to 10 minutes or until edges are lightly golden brown. Remove from cookie sheets to cooling racks. Cool completely, about 30 minutes.

4. Turn each cookie upside down to look like reindeer face. Outline cookie with chocolate icing; fill in and spread icing with toothpick. Attach candy eyes and mint for nose. Decorate with white icing to look like antlers. Let stand until set.

1 Cookie: Calories 310; Total Fat 14g (Saturated Fat 6g, Trans Fat 0g); Cholesterol 0mg; Sodium 220mg; Total Carbohydrate 48g (Dietary Fiber 0g); Protein 2g **Exchanges:** ½ Starch, 2½ Other Carbohydrate, 2½ Fat **Carbohydrate Choices:** 3

Brown Sugar Snowflakes

PREP TIME: **1 Hour 30 Minutes** • START TO FINISH: **3 Hours 30 Minutes** • **2½ dozen cookies**

COOKIES

¾	cup butter, softened
¾	cup packed brown sugar
1	egg
2¼	cups all-purpose flour
½	teaspoon baking soda
¼	teaspoon salt

FROSTING

1½	teaspoons meringue powder
1	tablespoon cold water
½	cup powdered sugar
	Granulated sugar, if desired

1. In large bowl, beat butter and brown sugar with electric mixer on medium-high speed until light and fluffy. Beat in egg until blended. On low speed, beat in flour, baking soda and salt.

2. Divide dough into 4 parts; shape each part into a flat round. Wrap each round separately in plastic wrap. Refrigerate 2 hours.

3. Heat oven to 350°F. Line cookie sheets with cooking parchment paper. Unwrap dough; on floured surface, roll 1 round at a time to ¼-inch thickness. Cut with floured snowflake-shaped cookie cutter. On cookie sheets, place cutouts 1 inch apart. Reroll scraps once, chilling dough again before cutting additional cookies.

4. Bake 8 to 11 minutes or until lightly browned. Remove from cookie sheets to cooling racks. Cool completely, about 30 minutes.

5. In medium bowl, beat meringue powder and cold water with electric mixer on medium speed until peaks form. Gradually beat in powdered sugar until soft peaks form, about 1 minute. Spoon frosting into decorating bag fitted with medium round tip; pipe frosting onto cookies. Sprinkle with granulated sugar. Let stand until set.

1 Cookie: Calories 110; Total Fat 5g (Saturated Fat 3g, Trans Fat 0g); Cholesterol 20mg; Sodium 80mg; Total Carbohydrate 15g (Dietary Fiber 0g); Protein 1g **Exchanges:** 1 Other Carbohydrate, 1 Fat **Carbohydrate Choices:** 1

Tinsel Time Tips

Roll dough between sheets of cooking parchment paper to keep it from sticking to the counter.

Use dark brown sugar for a little more molasses flavor.

Oatmeal Shortbread Santas

PREP TIME: **55 Minutes** • START TO FINISH: **1 Hour 40 Minutes** • **1 dozen cookies**

COOKIES

- ⅔ cup butter, softened
- ½ cup packed brown sugar
- 1 teaspoon vanilla
- 1 cup all-purpose flour
- ¾ cup quick-cooking oats
- ¼ teaspoon baking powder

FROSTING AND DECORATIONS

- 2 cans (6.4 oz each) white decorating icing
- 6 miniature marshmallows, cut in half
- 1 tablespoon red decorating sugar
- 24 blue mini candy-coated milk chocolate candies
- 12 red mini candy-coated chocolate candies

1. In large bowl, beat butter, brown sugar and vanilla with electric mixer on medium speed until creamy. Stir in flour, oats and baking powder. Shape dough into ball. Wrap in plastic wrap; refrigerate 30 minutes.

2. Heat oven to 350°F. On well-floured surface, roll dough until ¼-inch thickness. Cut with 3- to 3½-inch heart-shaped cookie cutter. On ungreased cookie sheet, place cutouts 2 inches apart.

3. Bake 8 to 10 minutes or until edges are light golden brown. Cool 1 minute; remove from cookie sheet to cooling rack. Cool completely.

4. Turn cookies so pointed ends are up. Using desired tip, pipe frosting on upper one-third of cookie for hat. Place 1 marshmallow half at tip of each hat; sprinkle with red sugar. Using small dots of frosting, attach 2 blue candies on each cookie for eyes. Pipe small frosting mustache below eyes; place red candy in center for mouth. Pipe frosting on lower one-third of each cookie for beard. Store in single layer, loosely covered.

1 Cookie: Calories 190; Total Fat 11g (Saturated Fat 7g, Trans Fat 0g); Cholesterol 25mg; Sodium 85mg; Total Carbohydrate 20g (Dietary Fiber 0g); Protein 2g **Exchanges:** 1 Starch, ½ Other Carbohydrate, 2 Fat **Carbohydrate Choices:** 1

Tinsel Time Tip

Use any small round blue and red candies for the eyes and noses.

Holiday House Cookies

PREP TIME: **1 Hour** • START TO FINISH: **1 Hour 30 Minutes** • **8 large cookies**

1   pouch Betty Crocker® gingerbread cookie mix

½   cup butter, softened

1   tablespoon water

1   egg

1   container (1 lb) creamy white or vanilla creamy ready-to-spread frosting, if desired

     Assorted small candies, if desired

1. Heat oven to 375°F. In medium bowl, stir cookie mix, butter, water and egg until dough forms. Divide dough in half.

2. On floured surface, roll half of dough at a time into 9x6-inch rectangle. Cut rectangle into 6 (3-inch) squares. Place 4 squares on ungreased cookie sheet. Cut remaining 2 squares diagonally in half to form 4 triangles. Place 1 triangle on one side of each square for roof; press dough to seal.

3. Bake 8 to 11 minutes or until set. Cool 5 minutes. Remove from cookie sheet to cooling rack. Cool completely, about 15 minutes. Decorate with frosting and candies.

1 Cookie (Undecorated): Calories 370; Total Fat 17g (Saturated Fat 9g, Trans Fat 0g); Cholesterol 55mg; Sodium 400mg; Total Carbohydrate 50g (Dietary Fiber 0g); Protein 3g **Exchanges:** 1 Starch, 2½ Other Carbohydrate, 3 Fat **Carbohydrate Choices:** 3

Tinsel Time Tips

Roll dough to an even thickness by rolling over two wooden dowels or rulers. Use dowels or rulers in the desired thickness, and place them on opposite sides of the dough.

For easy decorating, place the frosting in a resealable food-storage plastic bag, snip off a small corner of the bag and squeeze to frost.

Cinnamon Stars

COOKIES

1½	cups powdered sugar
1	cup butter, softened
1	egg
1	teaspoon vanilla
2½	cups all-purpose flour
1	teaspoon baking soda
1	teaspoon cream of tartar
1	teaspoon ground cinnamon

ICING

½	cup red cinnamon candies
½	cup water
2½	cups powdered sugar

1. In large bowl, beat 1½ cups powdered sugar and the butter with electric mixer on medium speed until smooth. Beat in egg and vanilla until smooth. Beat in flour, baking soda, cream of tartar and cinnamon until well blended. Cover; refrigerate 1 hour or until firm.

2. Heat oven to 375°F. Divide dough in half. On lightly floured surface, roll half of dough at a time to ¼-inch thickness. Cut with 2-inch star-shaped cookie cutter. On ungreased cookie sheets, place cutouts 1 inch apart.

3. Bake 7 to 8 minutes or until light golden. Cool 1 minute; remove from cookie sheets to cooling racks. Cool completely, about 30 minutes.

4. In 2-quart saucepan, heat candies and water to boiling over medium-high heat, stirring frequently. Reduce heat to medium-low; simmer uncovered 5 to 6 minutes, stirring frequently, until candies are melted. Remove from heat. With whisk, stir in 2½ cups powdered sugar, ½ cup at a time, until smooth. Drizzle icing over cookies. (Icing sets up quickly; if necessary, add water, 1 teaspoon at a time, for drizzling consistency.)

1 Cookie: Calories 50; Total Fat 2g (Saturated Fat 1g, Trans Fat 0g); Cholesterol 5mg; Sodium 25mg; Total Carbohydrate 9g (Dietary Fiber 0g); Protein 0g **Exchanges:** ½ Other Carbohydrate, ½ Fat **Carbohydrate Choices:** ½

Tinsel Time Tips

Wrap up these pretty glazed cookie stars with a cookie cutter along with the recipe so your friends can make their own.

If you're in a hurry, skip making the icing from scratch and use decorating icing instead.

Sparkling Lemon Snowflakes

PREP TIME: **50 Minutes** • START TO FINISH: **1 Hour 40 Minutes** • **6 dozen cookies**

COOKIES

¾	cup butter, softened
¾	cup granulated sugar
2	teaspoons grated lemon peel
1	egg
2¼	cups all-purpose flour
¼	teaspoon salt

GLAZE AND GARNISH

2	cups powdered sugar
2	tablespoons lemon juice
2	tablespoons water
¼	cup coarse white sparkling sugar

1. In large bowl, beat butter and granulated sugar with electric mixer on medium speed until light and fluffy. Add lemon peel and egg; beat until well blended. On low speed, gradually beat in flour and salt until well blended.

2. Heat oven to 350°F. On floured surface, roll dough to ⅛-inch thickness. Cut with lightly floured 2½- to 3-inch snowflake-shaped cookie cutter. On ungreased cookie sheets, place cutouts 2 inches apart.

3. Bake 8 to 10 minutes or until cookies just begin to brown. Remove from cookie sheets to cooling racks. Cool completely, about 10 minutes.

4. In small bowl, mix powdered sugar, lemon juice and water. Using small metal spatula, spread glaze on tops of cookies; sprinkle with sparkling sugar. When glaze is dry, store in airtight container.

1 Cookie: Calories 60; Total Fat 2g (Saturated Fat 1g, Trans Fat 0g); Cholesterol 10mg; Sodium 25mg; Total Carbohydrate 9g (Dietary Fiber 0g); Protein 0g **Exchanges:** ½ Other Carbohydrate, ½ Fat **Carbohydrate Choices:** ½

Tinsel Time Tip

If you don't have a snowflake-shaped cookie cutter, you can use either a star-shaped or scalloped-edge cutter and then cut small triangles and pieces out of the center to form snowflakes.

Lime Christmas Wreaths

PREP TIME: **1 Hour 10 Minutes** • START TO FINISH: **2 Hours 45 Minutes** • **2½ dozen cookies**

COOKIES

½	cup butter, softened
¼	cup sour cream
¾	cup granulated sugar
1	egg
2	tablespoons grated lime peel
1	tablespoon lime juice
1	teaspoon vanilla
2½	cups all-purpose flour
½	teaspoon baking soda
¼	teaspoon salt

GLAZE AND DECORATIONS

1	cup powdered sugar
2	to 3 tablespoons lime juice
	Colored sugars, if desired
	White or colored candy sprinkles, if desired

Tinsel Time Tips

If you prefer, you can skip the glaze, and sprinkle the unbaked cookies with colored sugar before baking. Some sprinkles will melt during baking, so do some experimenting before sprinkling all of the cookies.

1. In large bowl, beat butter, sour cream and granulated sugar with electric mixer on medium speed until creamy. Add egg, lime peel, lime juice and vanilla; beat until smooth. On low speed, beat in flour, baking soda and salt until dough forms. Divide dough in half; shape each half into a round. Wrap each in plastic wrap. Refrigerate 1 hour.

2. Heat oven to 375°F. Place pastry cloth on work surface; sprinkle with flour. With floured cloth-covered rolling pin, roll 1 round of dough to ⅛-inch thickness. Cut with floured 3-inch fluted cutter. With 1-inch scalloped or fluted canapé cutter, cut out center of each round. On ungreased cookie sheets, place wreath cutouts 1 inch apart. Cut each small cutout in half; brush backs of small cutouts with water and place on wreaths for bows. Repeat with second round of dough.

3. Bake 6 to 8 minutes or until edges start to brown. Remove from cookie sheets to cooling racks; cool completely, about 15 minutes.

4. In small bowl, mix powdered sugar and 2 tablespoons of the lime juice with whisk. Stir in remaining 1 tablespoon lime juice, 1 teaspoon at a time, until glaze is thin. Working with a few cookies at a time, brush glaze over cookies and immediately decorate with sugars and sprinkles. Let stand until set. Store between layers of waxed paper in tightly covered container.

1 Cookie: Calories 110; Total Fat 3.5g (Saturated Fat 2g, Trans Fat 0g); Cholesterol 15mg; Sodium 65mg; Total Carbohydrate 17g (Dietary Fiber 0g); Protein 1g **Exchanges:** ½ Starch, ½ Other Carbohydrate, ½ Fat **Carbohydrate Choices**: 1

Merry Molasses Cookies

PREP TIME: **45 Minutes** • START TO FINISH: **4 Hours 15 Minutes** • **About 3 dozen cookies**

COOKIES

1	cup granulated sugar
½	cup shortening
4	cups all-purpose flour
1	cup full-flavor (dark) molasses
½	cup water
1½	teaspoons salt
1	teaspoon baking soda
1½	teaspoons ground ginger
½	teaspoon ground cloves
½	teaspoon ground nutmeg
¼	teaspoon ground allspice

GLAZE, IF DESIRED

3	cups powdered sugar
⅓	cup butter, softened
½	teaspoon ground cinnamon
1½	teaspoons vanilla
2	to 3 tablespoons milk

1. In large bowl, beat granulated sugar and shortening with electric mixer on medium speed, or mix with spoon. Stir in remaining cookie ingredients. Cover; refrigerate dough at least 3 hours or until firm.

2. Heat oven to 375°F. Generously grease cookie sheets with shortening or cooking spray. On generously floured cloth-covered surface, roll half of dough at a time to ¼-inch thickness. Cut with 3-inch round cookie cutter. On cookie sheets, place cutouts about 1½ inches apart.

3. Bake 10 to 12 minutes or until almost no indentation remains when touched lightly in center. Cool 2 minutes; remove from cookie sheets to cooling racks. Cool completely, about 30 minutes.

4. In small bowl, mix glaze ingredients until smooth. Spread on cooled cookies.

1 Cookie: Calories 130; Total Fat 3g (Saturated Fat 0.5g, Trans Fat 0g); Cholesterol 0mg; Sodium 135mg; Total Carbohydrate 23g (Dietary Fiber 0g); Protein 1g **Exchanges:** ½ Starch, 1 Other Carbohydrate, ½ Fat **Carbohydrate Choices:** 1½

Tinsel Time Tips

Spread these cookies with glaze, then sprinkle unsweetened baking cocoa over a stencil to jazz them up for the holidays.

Mild-flavor (light) molasses or honey can be substituted for the dark molasses for a slightly different flavor.

Christmas Cookie Pops

PREP TIME: **25 Minutes** • START TO FINISH: **1 Hour 10 Minutes** • **1 dozen cookie pops**

1 pouch Betty Crocker sugar cookie mix

½ cup butter, softened

¼ cup all-purpose flour

1 egg

Green food color

12 wooden sticks with rounded ends

½ container (1 lb) creamy ready-to-spread frosting (any white variety)

Assorted decorations, as desired (see ideas below)

1. Heat oven to 375°F. In medium bowl, stir cookie mix, butter, flour and egg until dough forms. Divide dough in half. Stir green food color, 1 drop at a time, into part of dough used to make Christmas trees until desired color is reached.

2. On floured surface, roll each dough half to ¼-inch thickness. Cut green dough with 3½- to 5-inch Christmas tree cookie cutter; cut white dough with 3½- to 5-inch snowman cookie cutter. On ungreased cookie sheet, place cutouts 2 inches apart. Carefully insert a wooden stick into bottom of each cookie.

3. Bake 10 to 13 minutes or until edges are light golden brown. Cool 1 minute; remove from cookie sheet to cooling rack. Cool completely, about 30 minutes. Decorate as directed below.

Christmas Trees: Leave frosting white OR stir a few drops green food color into frosting if desired; spread baked cookies with frosting. Sprinkle with colored sugar. Press tiny candies into frosting for tree decorations. To make star for top of tree, flatten large yellow gumdrop by rolling with rolling pin; cut into star shape with sharp knife. Place on cookie.

Snowmen: Spread baked cookies with frosting. To make hat, flatten large black gumdrop by rolling with rolling pin; cut into hat shape with sharp knife. Place on cookie. To make scarf, cut long strip from any red variety chewy fruit-flavored snack roll; cut small slits into ends of scarf with scissors to look like fringe. Place around neck of snowman. Use raisins or candies for eyes, nose and buttons. Attach small unwrapped candy cane to snowman.

1 Cookie Pop: Calories 330; Total Fat 15g (Saturated Fat 6g, Trans Fat 3g); Cholesterol 40mg; Sodium 220mg; Total Carbohydrate 47g (Dietary Fiber 0g); Protein 2g **Exchanges:** 2 Starch, 1 Other Carbohydrate, 2½ Fat **Carbohydrate Choices:** 3

Coconut Snowmen Pops: Sprinkle coconut over frosted snowmen, one cookie at a time, while frosting is still wet.

Tinsel Time Tip

Serve these cookie pops from little holiday pots to make them even more tempting! Cut pieces of floral foam (available at craft stores) to fit snugly inside flowerpots to within 1½ inch of tops. Glue or tape foam pieces securely in pots. Carefully poke bottoms of sticks into foam. Cover foam with shredded coconut to look like snow.

Easy Drop
& Shaped

Raspberry Poinsettia Blossoms

PREP TIME: **25 Minutes** • START TO FINISH: **1 Hour 50 Minutes** • **3 dozen cookies**

¾ cup butter, softened

½ cup sugar

1 teaspoon vanilla

1 box (4-serving size) raspberry-flavored gelatin

1 egg

2 cups all-purpose flour

2 tablespoons yellow candy sprinkles

1. In large bowl, beat butter, sugar, vanilla, gelatin and egg with electric mixer on medium speed. On low speed, beat in flour. Cover with plastic wrap; refrigerate 1 hour.

2. Heat oven to 375°F. Shape dough into 36 (1¼-inch) balls. On ungreased cookie sheets, place balls about 2 inches apart. With sharp knife, make 6 cuts in top of each ball about three-fourths of the way through to make 6 wedges. Spread wedges apart slightly to form flower petals (cookies will separate and flatten as they bake). Sprinkle about ⅛ teaspoon candy sprinkles into center of each cookie.

3. Bake 9 to 11 minutes or until set. Cool 2 minutes; remove from cookie sheets to cooling rack.

1 Cookie: Calories 90; Total Fat 4g (Saturated Fat 2.5g, Trans Fat 0g); Cholesterol 15mg; Sodium 40mg; Total Carbohydrate 11g (Dietary Fiber 0g); Protein 1g **Exchanges:** 1 Other Carbohydrate, 1 Fat **Carbohydrate Choices:** 1

Tinsel Time Tip

For a flavor twist, use strawberry-, cranberry- or cherry-flavored gelatin instead of the raspberry.

Almond Tree Cookies

PREP TIME: **2 Hours** • START TO FINISH: **2 Hours** • **4 dozen cookies**

COOKIES

- 1   cup butter, softened
- ½   cup granulated sugar
- ½   teaspoon almond extract
- 2   cups all-purpose flour

FROSTING

- 1   cup powdered sugar
- 2   tablespoons butter, softened
- 1   to 2 tablespoons milk
- 8   to 10 drops green food color

1. Heat oven to 350°F. In medium bowl, beat 1 cup butter, the granulated sugar and almond extract with electric mixer on medium speed until smooth. On low speed, beat in flour.

2. Shape dough into 48 (1-inch) balls. On ungreased cookie sheets, place balls 2 inches apart.

3. Bake 12 to 15 minutes or until firm to the touch. Cool 1 minute; remove from cookie sheets to cooling racks. Cool completely, about 30 minutes.

4. In small bowl, beat powdered sugar, 2 tablespoons butter and the milk on medium speed until smooth and spreadable. Stir in green food color until uniform color.

5. Spoon frosting into resealable food-storage plastic bag. Seal bag; cut off tiny corner of bag. Squeeze bag to pipe tree shape in zigzag pattern on each cookie.

1 Cookie: Calories 80; Total Fat 4.5g (Saturated Fat 2.5g, Trans Fat 0g); Cholesterol 10mg; Sodium 30mg; Total Carbohydrate 9g (Dietary Fiber 0g); Protein 0g **Exchanges:** ½ Other Carbohydrate, 1 Fat **Carbohydrate Choices:** ½

Tinsel Time Tip

Add ornaments to the cookie trees by sprinkling with yellow, red and green holiday candy sprinkles. Candy stars on top of the trees are a nice touch.

Sugar Cookie Snowmen

PREP TIME: **1 Hour 30 Minutes** • START TO FINISH: **1 Hour 30 Minutes** • **21 cookies**

1 pouch Betty Crocker sugar cookie mix

2 tablespoons all-purpose flour

⅓ cup butter, softened

1 egg

21 pretzel sticks, broken in half

1 container (12 oz) fluffy white whipped ready-to-spread frosting

Assorted candies

1. Heat oven to 375°F. In medium bowl, stir cookie mix, flour, butter and egg until soft dough forms.

2. Shape dough into 21 (1¼-inch) balls, 21 (1-inch) balls and 21 (¾-inch) balls. For each snowman, place 3 balls in decreasing sizes with edges just touching on ungreased cookie sheet; flatten balls slightly. Place snowmen about 3 inches apart.

3. Bake 7 to 9 minutes or until edges are light golden brown. Remove from oven; immediately insert pretzel sticks into sides of middle balls for arms. Cool 5 minutes; remove from cookie sheet to cooling rack. Cool completely, about 15 minutes.

4. Frost cookies and decorate with candies.

1 Frosted Cookie (Undecorated): Calories 200; Total Fat 9g (Saturated Fat 3.5g, Trans Fat 2g); Cholesterol 20mg; Sodium 115mg; Total Carbohydrate 29g (Dietary Fiber 0g); Protein 1g **Exchanges:** ½ Starch, 1½ Other Carbohydrate, 1½ Fat **Carbohydrate Choices:** 2

Tinsel Time Tip

Sprinkle a serving platter with powdered sugar to look like snow and invite kids for some friendly finger licking.

Decorate-Before-You-Bake Cookies

PREP TIME: **50 Minutes** • START TO FINISH: **1 Hour 40 Minutes** • **6 dozen cookies**

COOKIES

¾ cup butter, softened

½ cup sugar

1 egg

1¾ cups all-purpose flour

½ teaspoon baking soda

¼ teaspoon cream of tartar

¼ teaspoon salt

DECORATING MIXTURE

½ cup butter, softened

3 teaspoons milk

½ cup all-purpose flour

4 drops red food color

4 drops green food color

2 tablespoons sugar

1. In large bowl, beat ¾ cup butter and ½ cup sugar with electric mixer on medium speed until light and fluffy. Add egg; beat well. Stir in 1¾ cups flour, the baking soda, cream of tartar and salt. Knead dough into smooth ball. Wrap in plastic wrap; refrigerate until firm, about 1 hour.

2. Meanwhile, in small bowl, mix ½ cup butter, the milk and ½ cup flour with fork until well mixed. Transfer half of mixture to second small bowl. Stir red food color into 1 half and green food color into other half. Spoon each mixture into decorating bag fitted with small writing tip; set aside.

3. Heat oven to 375°F. Divide dough in half. Shape 1 half of dough into 30 (¾-inch) balls. On ungreased cookie sheets, place balls 2 inches apart. In small bowl, place 2 tablespoons sugar. Dip bottom of glass into sugar and use to flatten each ball into 1½-inch round. Pipe colored mixture from decorating bags on each cookie in various holiday designs. Repeat with remaining half of dough.

4. Bake 7 to 9 minutes or until set. Immediately remove from cookie sheets to cooling racks.

1 Cookie: Calories 50; Total Fat 3.5g (Saturated Fat 2g, Trans Fat 0g); Cholesterol 10mg; Sodium 40mg; Total Carbohydrate 5g (Dietary Fiber 0g); Protein 0g **Exchanges:** ½ Other Carbohydrate, ½ Fat **Carbohydrate Choices:** ½

Tinsel Time Tip

If you don't have decorating bags and tips, use small resealable food-storage plastic bags. Cut off the tip of one corner for piping.

Easy Peppermint Candy Cookies

PREP TIME: **15 Minutes** • START TO FINISH: **1 Hour 10 Minutes** • **2½ dozen cookies**

1   pouch Betty Crocker sugar cookie mix

½   cup butter, softened

1   egg

¼   cup all-purpose flour

1   container (12 oz) fluffy white whipped ready-to-spread frosting

1   teaspoon peppermint extract

Red decorating sugar

1. Heat oven to 375°F. In large bowl, stir cookie mix, butter, egg and flour until dough forms. Shape dough into 30 (1¼-inch) balls. On ungreased cookie sheet, place balls 2 inches apart. Flatten slightly with bottom of glass.

2. Bake 8 to 10 minutes or until edges are light golden brown. Cool 1 minute; remove from cookie sheet to cooling rack. Cool completely, about 20 minutes.

3. In small bowl, mix frosting and peppermint extract. Spread each cookie with frosting. Using small spoon, sprinkle red sugar onto cookies in spiral design to look like peppermint candies.

1 Cookie: Calories 160; Total Fat 8g (Saturated Fat 3g, Trans Fat 0g); Cholesterol 15mg; Sodium 75mg; Total Carbohydrate 21g (Dietary Fiber 0g); Protein 0g **Exchanges:** 1½ Other Carbohydrate, 1½ Fat **Carbohydrate Choices:** 1½

Tinsel Time Tips

Spoon sugar into a resealable food-storage plastic bag. Snip off a corner of the bag and squeeze to sprinkle sugar over the frosted cookies.

Use green sugar in place of the red, if you'd like.

Jolly Snowman Faces

PREP TIME: **1 Hour** • START TO FINISH: **1 Hour 15 Minutes** • **2 dozen cookies**

1   pouch Betty Crocker sugar
    cookie mix

½   cup butter, softened

1   egg

1   container (12 oz) fluffy white
    whipped ready-to-spread
    frosting

    Red string licorice

    Assorted candies

1. Heat oven to 375°F. In medium bowl, stir cookie mix, butter and egg until soft dough forms. Onto ungreased cookie sheets, drop dough by rounded tablespoonfuls 2 inches apart.

2. Bake 11 to 14 minutes or until edges are light golden brown. Cool 1 minute; remove from cookie sheets to cooling racks. Cool completely, about 15 minutes.

3. Frost and decorate 1 cookie at a time. After spreading frosting on cookie, add licorice for band of earmuffs and candies for ear "covers" and snowman face.

1 Frosted Cookie (Undecorated): Calories 200; Total Fat 9g (Saturated Fat 4g, Trans Fat 2g); Cholesterol 20mg; Sodium 105mg; Total Carbohydrate 29g (Dietary Fiber 0g); Protein 1g
Exchanges: ½ Starch, 1½ Other Carbohydrate, 1½ Fat **Carbohydrate Choices:** 2

Tinsel Time Tip

Bake the cookies before hosting a holiday party, and
then let partygoers do the decorating.

Red Velvet
Rich-and-Creamy Cookies

PREP TIME: **1 Hour 10 Minutes** • START TO FINISH: **1 Hour 10 Minutes** • **3 dozen cookies**

1   pouch Betty Crocker sugar cookie mix

⅓   cup unsweetened baking cocoa

¼   cup butter, softened

¼   cup sour cream

1   tablespoon red food color

1   egg

¾   to 1 cup cream cheese creamy ready-to-spread frosting (from a 1-lb container)

¼   cup chopped nuts

1. Heat oven to 375°F. In large bowl, stir cookie mix, cocoa, butter, sour cream, food color and egg until soft dough forms.

2. Shape dough into 36 (1-inch) balls. On ungreased cookie sheets, place balls 2 inches apart.

3. Bake 8 to 9 minutes or until set. Cool 2 minutes; remove from cookie sheets to cooling racks. Cool completely, about 15 minutes.

4. Spread cookies with frosting. Sprinkle with nuts. Store tightly covered at room temperature.

1 Cookie: Calories 100; Total Fat 4.5g (Saturated Fat 1.5g, Trans Fat 1g); Cholesterol 10mg; Sodium 65mg; Total Carbohydrate 15g (Dietary Fiber 0g); Protein 1g **Exchanges:** ½ Starch, ½ Other Carbohydrate, 1 Fat **Carbohydrate Choices:** 1

Tinsel Time Tips

For even baking, make sure cookies are the same shape and size.

Be sure to use unsweetened baking cocoa found in the baking aisle for these cookies. Hot cocoa mix will be too sweet.

Chocolate-Cherry Pinwheels

PREP TIME: **1 Hour 15 Minutes** • START TO FINISH: **4 Hours 30 Minutes** • **About 4½ dozen cookies**

¾ cup butter, softened

1 cup sugar

2 eggs

3 cups all-purpose flour

1 teaspoon baking powder

½ teaspoon salt

1½ teaspoons almond extract

¼ cup maraschino cherries, finely chopped, drained on paper towels

3 drops red food color

1 teaspoon vanilla

1 tablespoon milk

¼ cup unsweetened baking cocoa

1. In large bowl, beat butter, sugar and eggs with electric mixer on medium speed until smooth. Beat in flour, baking powder and salt until well blended. Place half of dough in another medium bowl.

2. Beat almond extract, cherries and food color into half of dough. Divide cherry dough in half. Wrap each half in plastic wrap; refrigerate about 45 minutes or until firm.

3. Meanwhile, beat vanilla, milk and cocoa into remaining plain dough. Divide chocolate dough in half. Wrap each half in plastic wrap; refrigerate about 45 minutes or until firm.

4. Place one part of chocolate dough between 2 sheets of waxed paper; roll into 10x7-inch rectangle. Repeat with one part of cherry dough. Refrigerate both about 30 minutes or until firm. Peel top sheets of waxed paper from both doughs. Turn cherry dough upside down onto chocolate dough; starting at long side, roll up doughs together into a log. Wrap in plastic wrap; refrigerate 2 hours. Repeat with remaining parts of dough.

5. Heat oven to 350°F. Cut rolls of dough into ¼-inch slices with sharp knife. On ungreased cookie sheets, place slices 1 inch apart.

6. Bake 8 to 11 minutes or until surface appears dull. Remove from cookie sheets to cooling racks.

1 Cookie: Calories 70; Total Fat 3g (Saturated Fat 1.5g, Trans Fat 0g); Cholesterol 15mg; Sodium 55mg; Total Carbohydrate 10g (Dietary Fiber 0g); Protein 1g **Exchanges:** ½ Starch, ½ Fat **Carbohydrate Choices:** ½

Tinsel Time Tip

Cookie dough rolls can be wrapped and refrigerated for up to 24 hours before baking. To freeze cookie dough rolls, wrap in foil or freezerproof wrap. To thaw, let dough stand 15 to 30 minutes until easy to cut into slices.

Striped Peppermint Cookies

1   cup butter, softened

1   cup sugar

1   egg

½   teaspoon peppermint
    extract

2¼ cups all-purpose flour

¼   teaspoon salt

1   teaspoon red paste
    food color

1. Line 8x4-inch loaf pan with plastic wrap, leaving 1 inch of plastic wrap overhanging at 2 opposite sides of pan. In large bowl, beat butter and sugar with electric mixer on medium speed until light and fluffy. Beat in egg and peppermint extract. On medium-low speed, beat in flour and salt until blended.

2. Divide dough in half. Tint half of dough with red food color, kneading with gloved hands until well blended. Press half of plain dough evenly in bottom of pan. Gently press half of red dough evenly over plain dough. Repeat layers with remaining dough. Cover with plastic wrap; refrigerate 2 hours or until firm.

3. Heat oven to 350°F. Remove dough from loaf pan; unwrap. Cut dough in half lengthwise. Cut each half crosswise into ¼-inch slices. On ungreased cookie sheets, place slices 2 inches apart. Bake 10 to 12 minutes or until set. Cool 2 minutes; remove from cookie sheets to cooling racks.

1 Cookie: Calories 60; Total Fat 3g (Saturated Fat 2g, Trans Fat 3g); Cholesterol 0mg; Sodium 40mg; Total Carbohydrate 7g (Dietary Fiber 0g); Protein 1g **Exchanges:** ½ Starch, ½ Fat **Carbohydrate Choices:** ½

Tinsel Time Tip

To make checkerboard cookies, cut the dough lengthwise into quarters. Stack the slices to create a checkerboard pattern, then cut into ¼-inch slices.

Easy Spritz Cookies

PREP TIME: **45 Minutes** • START TO FINISH: **45 Minutes** • **4 dozen cookies**

1 pouch Betty Crocker sugar cookie mix

½ cup all-purpose flour

½ cup butter, melted

1 teaspoon almond extract

1 egg

Candy sprinkles and colored decorating sugars, if desired

Coarse white sugar

1. Heat oven to 375°F. In large bowl, stir cookie mix, flour, melted butter, extract and egg until soft dough forms.

2. Fit desired template in cookie press; fill cookie press with dough. Force dough through template onto ungreased cookie sheets. Sprinkle with sprinkles or decorating sugars.

3. Bake 6 to 8 minutes or until set but not brown. Cool 1 minute; remove from cookie sheets to cooling racks.

1 Cookie: Calories 70; Total Fat 3g (Saturated Fat 1g, Trans Fat 0g); Cholesterol 10mg; Sodium 40mg; Total Carbohydrate 10g (Dietary Fiber 0g); Protein 0g **Exchanges:** 1 Other Carbohydrate, ½ Fat **Carbohydrate Choices:** ½

Easy Snowy Spritz Cookies: Combine ½ cup powdered sugar, 1½ teaspoons milk and ¼ teaspoon rum extract; drizzle over baked and cooled cookies.

Tinsel Time Tip

Create holiday colors by tinting the dough with red or green food color before placing it in the cookie press.

Almond Angel Cookies

PREP TIME: **1 Hour** • START TO FINISH: **3 Hours 45 Minutes** • **4 dozen cookies**

COOKIES

1	cup butter, softened
1	cup sugar
2	tablespoons milk
1	teaspoon vanilla
½	teaspoon almond extract
¼	teaspoon salt
2½	cups all-purpose flour
2	tablespoons yellow decorating sugar
2	tablespoons blue decorating sugar
96	small pretzel twists
2	tablespoons sliced almonds

ICING

1	tube (4.25 oz) yellow decorating icing
1	tube (4.25 oz) pink decorating icing

1. In large bowl, beat butter with electric mixer on medium-high speed until light and fluffy. Add sugar; beat until creamy, scraping bowl frequently. Stir in milk, vanilla, almond extract and salt. Stir in flour until well mixed.

2. Measure ½ cup of dough into resealable food-storage plastic bag; refrigerate. Divide remaining dough in half; roll each into a 6-inch log. Roll 1 log in yellow sugar; roll second log in blue sugar. Wrap logs separately in plastic wrap or waxed paper. Chill until firm, at least 2 hours.

3. Heat oven to 350°F. For each cookie, place 2 pretzels with flat sides touching on ungreased large cookie sheets, 3 inches apart. Cut dough logs into 48 (¼-inch) slices. (If dough cracks, allow to sit at room temperature a few minutes.) To make angel body, fold in opposite sides at top of each slice to make triangular-shaped body; place each slice on top of 2 pretzels so double loops of pretzels form angel wings at each side. Press lightly into pretzels. Using reserved dough from plastic bag, roll ½ teaspoon dough into ball; place on top for head of each angel. Press 2 sliced almonds into dough to make song book. Repeat to make 48 cookies.

4. Bake 11 to 14 minutes or until edges are firm and just begin to brown. Cool 2 to 3 minutes. Remove from cookie sheets to cooling racks. Cool completely, about 15 minutes.

5. Pipe yellow icing on cooled cookies to make eyes and hair. Pipe pink icing to make mouths. Let stand until frosting is set.

1 Cookie: Calories 100; Total Fat 4g (Saturated Fat 2.5g, Trans Fat 0g); Cholesterol 10mg; Sodium 70mg; Total Carbohydrate 14g (Dietary Fiber 0g); Protein 1g **Exchanges:** 1 Other Carbohydrate, 1 Fat **Carbohydrate Choices:** 1

Pecan-Shortbread Trees

PREP TIME: **30 Minutes** • START TO FINISH: **1 Hour 15 Minutes** • **32 cookies**

1 cup butter, softened

⅔ cup powdered sugar

½ teaspoon vanilla

5 drops green food color

1¾ cups all-purpose flour

½ cup coarsely chopped pecans

32 pecan halves

¾ cup white vanilla baking chips

Granulated sugar, if desired

32 yellow candy stars, if desired

1. Heat oven to 325°F. Spray or lightly grease 2 large cookie sheets. In large bowl, beat butter and powdered sugar with electric mixer on medium speed until light and fluffy. Beat in vanilla and food color. On low speed, beat in flour just until mixed. Stir in chopped pecans.

2. Divide dough into 4 equal parts; shape each into ball. Place 2 balls of dough on each cookie sheet, on opposite ends. With rolling pin or floured fingers, gently flatten and shape each ball into 6-inch round. With large knife, divide and cut each round into 8 wedges, slightly separating each cut with knife. Poke tops of wedges with fork, and place 1 pecan half in middle of each outer edge to make tree trunk.

3. Bake 15 to 18 minutes or until firm but not brown. While still warm, cut into wedges again. Cool completely on cookie sheets, about 30 minutes.

4. Place cooled tree wedges on cooling racks or waxed paper. Place baking chips in small microwavable bowl. Microwave on High 40 to 60 seconds, stirring every 20 seconds. Spoon into small resealable food-storage plastic bag. Cut small tip off 1 corner of bag, and drizzle side to side over wedges to make tree garland. Sprinkle with sugar. Top each tree with star.

1 Cookie: Calories 160; Total Fat 11g (Saturated Fat 6g, Trans Fat 0g); Cholesterol 15mg; Sodium 65mg; Total Carbohydrate 15g (Dietary Fiber 0g); Protein 1g **Exchanges:** 1 Starch, 2 Fat **Carbohydrate Choices:** 1

Tinsel Time Tips

After the holiday season, make these cookies without the food color, pecan "trunks" and stars.

If using paste food color instead of the liquid, you need only a small amount to get a nice green color.

Ginger-Lemon Delights

PREP TIME: **50 Minutes** • START TO FINISH: **1 Hour 10 Minutes** • **3 dozen cookies**

COOKIES

1	pouch Betty Crocker sugar cookie mix
½	cup shortening
¼	cup mild-flavor (light) molasses
1	tablespoon ground ginger
1¼	teaspoons ground cinnamon
1	teaspoon ground cloves
1	egg

GLAZE AND GARNISH

1	cup powdered sugar
1	teaspoon grated lemon peel
4	teaspoons lemon juice
¼	cup finely chopped crystallized ginger

1. Heat oven to 375°F. In medium bowl, stir cookie mix, shortening, molasses, ginger, cinnamon, cloves and egg until very soft dough forms.

2. Onto ungreased cookie sheets, drop dough by tablespoonfuls about 2 inches apart.

3. Bake 8 to 10 minutes. Cool; remove from cookie sheets to cooling racks. Cool completely, about 15 minutes.

4. In small bowl, stir powdered sugar, lemon peel and lemon juice until smooth. Spread glaze on cookies. Sprinkle with crystallized ginger.

1 Cookie: Calories 110; Total Fat 4.5g (Saturated Fat 1g, Trans Fat 1g); Cholesterol 5mg; Sodium 45mg; Total Carbohydrate 18g (Dietary Fiber 0g); Protein 0g **Exchanges:** 1 Other Carbohydrate, 1 Fat **Carbohydrate Choices:** 1

Ginger-Orange Delights: In step 4, substitute orange peel and orange juice for lemon peel and lemon juice.

Holiday Snickerdoodles

PREP TIME: **30 Minutes** • START TO FINISH: **1 Hour 30 Minutes** • **3 dozen cookies**

1 pouch Betty Crocker sugar cookie mix

⅓ cup butter, melted

1 egg

2 tablespoons all-purpose flour

¼ cup sugar

1 teaspoon ground cinnamon

Red and green decorating icings (from 4.25-oz tubes)

1. Heat oven to 375°F. In large bowl, stir cookie mix, butter, egg and flour until soft dough forms.

2. In small bowl, mix sugar and cinnamon. Shape dough into 36 (1-inch) balls; roll in sugar-cinnamon mixture. On ungreased cookie sheets, place balls 2 inches apart.

3. Bake 11 to 12 minutes or until set. Cool 2 minutes; remove from cookie sheets to cooling racks. If desired, roll tops of warm cookies in remaining sugar-cinnamon mixture. Cool completely, about 30 minutes. Decorate as desired with icings. Let stand until set.

1 Cookie: Calories 80; Total Fat 3g (Saturated Fat 1.5g, Trans Fat 0.5g); Cholesterol 10mg; Sodium 45mg; Total Carbohydrate 13g (Dietary Fiber 0g); Protein 0g **Exchanges:** 1 Other Carbohydrate, ½ Fat **Carbohydrate Choices:** 1

Tinsel Time Tips

This cookie dough can be covered and refrigerated up to 24 hours before baking.

Instead of the decorating icing, decorate these cookies with fluffy white whipped ready-to-spread frosting, mixing one half with green food color and the other with red food color.

Cardamom Sugar Crisps

PREP TIME: **50 Minutes** • START TO FINISH: **2 Hours** • **4 dozen cookies**

COOKIES

¾	cup butter, softened
¾	cup packed brown sugar
½	teaspoon vanilla
1	egg
1½	cups all-purpose flour
1	teaspoon ground cardamom
¼	teaspoon salt
¼	teaspoon ground cinnamon
	Granulated sugar

GLAZE AND GARNISH

1½	cups powdered sugar
1	teaspoon vanilla
2	to 3 tablespoons milk
3	tablespoons white decorator sugar crystals

1. In large bowl, beat butter, brown sugar, ½ teaspoon vanilla and the egg with electric mixer on medium speed until smooth. On low speed, beat in flour, cardamom, salt and cinnamon. Cover with plastic wrap; refrigerate 1 hour.

2. Heat oven to 350°F. Shape dough into 48 (1-inch) balls. On ungreased cookie sheets, place balls 2 inches apart. Dip bottom of drinking glass into granulated sugar. Gently press sugared glass onto dough; flatten balls to about 1½ inches in diameter.

3. Bake 7 to 9 minutes or until edges are lightly browned. Immediately remove from cookie sheets to cooling racks. Cool completely, about 30 minutes.

4. In small bowl, mix powdered sugar, 1 teaspoon vanilla and enough of the milk until glaze is smooth and thin enough to drizzle. Drizzle glaze over cookies. Sprinkle with sugar crystals. Let stand until set.

1 Cookie: Calories 80; Total Fat 3g (Saturated Fat 2g, Trans Fat 0g); Cholesterol 10mg; Sodium 35mg; Total Carbohydrate 12g (Dietary Fiber 0g); Protein 0g **Exchanges:** 1 Other Carbohydrate, ½ Fat **Carbohydrate Choices:** 1

Tinsel Time Tip

Cardamom, one of the oldest spices in the world, is often used in cookies and other desserts and comes from the seeds of a ginger-like plant.

Best-Ever Chewy Gingerbread Cookies

PREP TIME: **1 Hour 30 Minutes** • START TO FINISH: **3 Hours 30 Minutes** • **7½ dozen cookies**

1	cup plus 2 tablespoons unsalted butter, softened
1	cup packed brown sugar
1	egg
¼	cup plus 2 tablespoons molasses
2½	cups all-purpose flour
2¼	teaspoons baking soda
½	teaspoon kosher (coarse) salt
1	tablespoon ground ginger
1	tablespoon ground cinnamon
2	teaspoons ground cloves
1½	teaspoons ground nutmeg
½	teaspoon ground allspice
⅔	cup granulated or coarse sugar

1. In large bowl, beat butter and brown sugar with electric mixer on medium speed until light and fluffy, about 5 minutes. Beat in egg and molasses. Stir in remaining ingredients except granulated sugar. Cover; refrigerate at least 2 hours.

2. Heat oven to 350°F. Line cookie sheets with cooking parchment paper. In small bowl, place granulated sugar. Shape dough into 90 (1-inch) balls; roll in sugar. On cookie sheets, place balls 2 inches apart.

3. Bake 8 to 10 minutes or just until set and soft in center. Cool 2 minutes; remove from cookie sheets to cooling racks. Store tightly covered up to 1 week.

1 Cookie: Calories 50; Total Fat 2.5g (Saturated Fat 1.5g, Trans Fat 0g); Cholesterol 10mg; Sodium 45mg; Total Carbohydrate 8g (Dietary Fiber 0g); Protein 0g **Exchanges:** ½ Other Carbohydrate, ½ Fat **Carbohydrate Choices:** ½

Tinsel Time Tip

You can use light or dark molasses in this recipe.

Italian Pignoli Nut Cookies

PREP TIME: **1 Hour** • START TO FINISH: **1 Hour 20 Minutes** • **3 dozen cookies**

1   pouch Betty Crocker sugar cookie mix

½   cup granulated sugar

½   cup butter, softened

1   can (8 oz) or 1 package (7 oz) almond paste, crumbled into ½-inch pieces

1   egg

2   cups pine nuts (8 oz)

1   tablespoon powdered sugar

1. Heat oven to 350°F. Line cookie sheet with cooking parchment paper.

2. In large bowl, beat cookie mix, granulated sugar, butter, almond paste and egg with electric mixer on low speed until soft dough forms. Shape dough by tablespoonfuls into 36 balls. Roll each ball in pine nuts, pressing to coat. On cookie sheet, place balls 2 inches apart.

3. Bake 13 to 17 minutes or just until edges are light golden brown. Cool 5 minutes; remove from cookie sheet to cooling rack. Cool completely, about 15 minutes. Sprinkle with powdered sugar.

1 Cookie: Calories 170; Total Fat 10g (Saturated Fat 2.5g, Trans Fat 0.5g); Cholesterol 15mg; Sodium 60mg; Total Carbohydrate 18g (Dietary Fiber 0g); Protein 2g **Exchanges:** ½ Starch, ½ Other Carbohydrate, 2 Fat **Carbohydrate Choices:** 1

Tinsel Time Tip

Look for budget-priced pine nuts (pignoli nuts) in the bulk-foods section of the grocery store or in club stores.

Russian Tea Cakes

PREP TIME: **1 Hour** • START TO FINISH: **1 Hour 25 Minutes** • **4 dozen cookies**

1   cup butter, softened
½   cup powdered sugar
1   teaspoon gluten-free vanilla
1   egg
2¼ cups Bisquick Gluten Free mix
¾   cup finely chopped nuts
⅔   cup powdered sugar

1. Heat oven to 400°F. In large bowl, mix butter, ½ cup powdered sugar, the vanilla and egg. Stir in Bisquick mix and nuts until dough holds together.

2. Shape dough into 48 (1-inch) balls. On ungreased cookie sheets, place balls about 1 inch apart.

3. Bake 9 to 11 minutes or until set but not brown. Immediately remove from cookie sheets to cooling racks. Cool slightly.

4. Roll warm cookies in powdered sugar; place on cooling racks to cool completely. Roll in powdered sugar again.

1 Cookie: Calories 80; Total Fat 5g (Saturated Fat 2.5g, Trans Fat 0g); Cholesterol 15mg; Sodium 90mg; Total Carbohydrate 8g (Dietary Fiber 0g); Protein 0g **Exchanges:** ½ Starch, 1 Fat **Carbohydrate Choices:** ½

Tinsel Time Tips

These rich little cookies are extra-special when made with macadamia nuts.

Cooking gluten free? Always read labels to make sure each recipe ingredient is gluten free. Products and ingredient sources can change.

Christmas Ball Cookies

PREP TIME: **50 Minutes** • START TO FINISH: **1 Hour 50 Minutes** • **2 dozen sandwich cookies**

COOKIES

1	cup butter, softened
½	cup powdered sugar
⅛	teaspoon salt
¼	teaspoon almond extract
2	cups all-purpose flour
	Red, green and white sanding sugar

FILLING

¼	cup butter, softened
1	cup powdered sugar
¼	teaspoon almond extract
1	tablespoon milk

1. In large bowl, beat 1 cup butter, ½ cup powdered sugar and the salt with electric mixer on medium speed about 2 minutes or until creamy. Beat in ¼ teaspoon almond extract. On low speed, beat in flour just until combined. Cover; refrigerate 30 minutes.

2. Heat oven to 350°F. Line cookie sheets with cooking parchment paper. Shape dough into 48 (¾-inch) balls. Roll 16 balls in each color of sanding sugar, coating completely. On cookie sheets, place balls 1 inch apart.

3. Bake 15 minutes or until set and bottoms are light golden brown. Remove from cookie sheets to cooling racks. Cool completely, about 30 minutes.

4. In small bowl, beat ¼ cup butter, 1 cup powdered sugar, ¼ teaspoon almond extract and the milk with electric mixer on medium speed until smooth. For each sandwich cookie, spread about ½ teaspoon filling on bottom of 1 cookie; top with second cookie, bottom side down, to form ball.

1 Sandwich Cookie: Calories 161; Total Fat 10g (Saturated Fat 6g); Sodium 97mg; Total Carbohydrate 18g (Dietary Fiber 0g); Protein 1g **Exchanges:** ½ Starch, ½ Other Carbohydrate, 2 Fat **Carbohydrate Choices:** 1

Tinsel Time Tips

Be sure to use butter for this recipe. And for the best results, carefully measure flour and powdered sugar by lightly spooning into a measuring cup and leveling off.

You may omit the filling for these sandwich cookies and simply serve them as colorful sugar cookies.

Baked Hazelnut Truffles

PREP TIME: **1 Hour** • START TO FINISH: **2 Hours** • **3½ dozen cookies**

4 oz semisweet baking chocolate

¼ cup butter

1 can (14 oz) sweetened condensed milk (not evaporated)

2 tablespoons hazelnut liqueur

2½ cups all-purpose flour

½ cup chopped hazelnuts (filberts)

40 milk chocolate stars

½ cup white vanilla baking chips

1 teaspoon vegetable oil

Candy sprinkles, if desired

1. Heat oven to 350°F. In large microwavable bowl, microwave baking chocolate and butter uncovered on Medium (50%) 2 to 3 minutes, stirring once, until softened. Stir in condensed milk, liqueur, flour and hazelnuts. Cover and refrigerate until firm, about 30 minutes.

2. Shape dough by tablespoonfuls around each chocolate star. On ungreased cookie sheet, place cookies 1 inch apart.

3. Bake 7 to 8 minutes or until dough is shiny and set but still soft. Cool 5 minutes; remove from cookie sheet to cooling rack. Cool about 30 minutes.

4. In small microwavable bowl, microwave white vanilla baking chips and oil uncovered on Medium (50%) 1 minute to 1 minute 15 seconds, stirring once, until softened. Stir until smooth. Dip top of each cookie into melted mixture; immediately top each with candy sprinkles while mixture is still soft. Let stand until coating is set.

1 Cookie: Calories 100; Total Fat 5g (Saturated Fat 2.5g, Trans Fat 0g); Cholesterol 0mg; Sodium 20mg; Total Carbohydrate 13g (Dietary Fiber 0g); Protein 1g **Exchanges:** 1 Other Carbohydrate, 1 Fat **Carbohydrate Choices:** 1

Tinsel Time Tip

For a gift, tuck single cookies in small tissue-lined holiday boxes.

Chocolate-Cherry Snowballs

PREP TIME: **1 Hour 25 Minutes** • START TO FINISH: **2 Hours 5 Minutes** • **About 4 dozen cookies**

1   cup butter, softened

1   cup powdered sugar

½   teaspoon almond extract

2   cups all-purpose flour

¼   teaspoon salt

1   cup (8 oz) candied cherries, finely chopped

½   cup dark chocolate chips

1. Heat oven to 400°F. In large bowl, beat butter with electric mixer on medium speed until fluffy. Gradually beat in ½ cup of the powdered sugar until light and fluffy. Stir in almond extract. In medium bowl, mix flour and salt. On low speed, beat flour mixture into butter mixture until well blended. Stir in cherries.

2. Shape dough into 48 (1-inch) balls. On ungreased cookie sheet, place balls 2 inches apart.

3. Bake 9 to 11 minutes or until edges just begin to brown. Cool slightly. In small bowl, place remaining ½ cup powdered sugar. Roll each cookie in powdered sugar. Place on cooling rack to cool completely.

4. Place chocolate chips in small microwavable bowl. Microwave on High 45 to 60 seconds, stirring every 20 seconds. Stir until chips are melted and smooth. Spoon melted chips into small resealable food-storage plastic bag. Cut small tip off 1 corner of bag, and drizzle over cooled cookies. Let stand at room temperature at least 30 minutes until chocolate hardens before storing.

1 Cookie: Calories 90; Total Fat 4.5g (Saturated Fat 3g, Trans Fat 0g); Cholesterol 10mg; Sodium 45mg; Total Carbohydrate 11g (Dietary Fiber 0g); Protein 0g **Exchanges:** 1 Other Carbohydrate, 1 Fat **Carbohydrate Choices:** 1

Tinsel Time Tips

To make it easier to chop the cherries, dip a knife in water or use a kitchen scissors sprayed with cooking spray.

Refrigerate cookies 10 minutes to reduce cooling time and set the chocolate faster.

Peanut Butter Reindeer Cookies

PREP TIME: **50 Minutes** • START TO FINISH: **50 Minutes** • **2 dozen cookies**

1   pouch Betty Crocker peanut
    butter cookie mix

3   tablespoons vegetable oil

1   tablespoon water

1   egg

2   tablespoons sugar

72 semisweet chocolate chips
    (about 3 tablespoons)

12 star-shaped Christmas
    pretzels or pretzel sticks

1. Heat oven to 375°F. In medium bowl, mix cookies as directed on package, using oil, water and egg.

2. Shape dough into 24 (1¼-inch) balls. On ungreased cookie sheets, place balls 2 inches apart. Dip bottom of drinking glass in sugar; press each ball until to ½-inch thickness.

3. Pinch bottom edge of each cookie to form a longer point. At point of each cookie, place 1 chocolate chip for nose; press down slightly. Place 2 chocolate chips on each cookie for eyes; press down slightly. With small sharp knife, cut star points from Christmas pretzels to form 48 small V-shaped pretzels (if using pretzel sticks, cut into quarters). Press 2 pretzel pieces into top of each cookie for antlers.

4. Bake 9 to 11 minutes or until edges begin to brown. Remove from cookie sheets to cooling racks.

1 Cookie: Calories 120; Total Fat 5g (Saturated Fat 1.5g, Trans Fat 0g); Cholesterol 10mg; Sodium 115mg; Total Carbohydrate 16g (Dietary Fiber 0g); Protein 2g **Exchanges:** ½ Starch, ½ Other Carbohydrate, 1 Fat **Carbohydrate Choices:** 1

Tinsel Time Tips

These are easy cookies for kids to help with. Let them each create their own herd of reindeer.

You can use small candies instead of chocolate chips to decorate the cookies. Do a test bake to see if they hold up to baking temperature. If not, just attach them to the baked cookies with a little melted chocolate.

Festive Peanut Butter Blossom Cookies

PREP TIME: **1 Hour** • START TO FINISH: **1 Hour** • **3 dozen cookies**

1 pouch Betty Crocker peanut butter cookie mix

3 tablespoons vegetable oil

1 tablespoon water

1 egg

Sugar

36 Hershey's® Kisses® brand milk chocolates, unwrapped

White decorating gel

Holiday candy sprinkles

Red decorating icing

1. Heat oven to 375°F. In medium bowl, stir cookie mix, oil, water and egg until dough forms.

2. Shape dough into 36 (1-inch balls); roll in sugar. On ungreased cookie sheets, place balls 2 inches apart.

3. Bake 10 to 12 minutes or until light golden brown. Immediately press 1 chocolate in center of each cookie. Remove from cookie sheets to cooling racks. Cool completely, about 20 minutes. Decorate as desired using remaining ingredients.

1 Cookie: Calories 100; Total Fat 5g (Saturated Fat 2g, Trans Fat 0g); Cholesterol 5mg; Sodium 75mg; Total Carbohydrate 14g (Dietary Fiber 0g); Protein 2g **Exchanges:** ½ Starch, ½ Other Carbohydrate, 1 Fat **Carbohydrate Choices:** 1

The HERSHEY'S® KISSES® trademark and trade dress and the Conical figure and plume device are used under license.

Tinsel Time Tip

The cookie dough can be covered and refrigerated up to 24 hours before baking. If it's too firm to work with, let it stand at room temperature 30 minutes.

Reindeer Peanut Butter Pops

PREP TIME: **55 Minutes** • START TO FINISH: **3 Hours 25 Minutes** • **About 28 cookie pops**

COOKIES

- ½ cup granulated sugar
- ½ cup packed brown sugar
- ½ cup creamy peanut butter
- ½ cup butter, softened
- 1 egg
- 1½ cups all-purpose flour
- ¾ teaspoon baking soda
- ½ teaspoon baking powder

DECORATIONS

- 28 wooden sticks with rounded ends, if desired
- 56 small pretzel twists
- 1 oz semisweet baking chocolate
- ½ teaspoon shortening
- 56 candy-coated chocolate candies
- 28 candy-coated chocolate candies or cinnamon candies

1. In large bowl, beat sugars, peanut butter, butter and egg with electric mixer on medium speed, or mix with spoon. Stir in flour, baking soda and baking powder.

2. Wrap dough in plastic wrap, leaving ends open. Roll dough into 7-inch log. Pinch along top of log and plastic to form one corner of triangle. Roll log over; pinch again to form second corner. Roll log over; pinch again to form third corner. Straighten sides of log to form a triangular-shaped log. Close ends of plastic wrap; refrigerate at least 2 hours.

3. Heat oven to 375°F. Unwrap log; cut into ¼-inch slices. Insert 1 inch of wooden stick into corner of each cookie. On ungreased cookie sheet, place slices about 2 inches apart. Reshape cookies if necessary. Insert 2 pretzels into top of each cookie slice for antlers. Bake 6 to 8 minutes or until edges are firm. Cool 1 minute; remove from cookie sheet to cooling rack. Cool completely.

4. Line plate with waxed paper. In small microwavable bowl, place chocolate and shortening. Microwave uncovered on Medium (50%) 3 to 4 minutes, stirring after 2 minutes, until mixture is smooth. Using tweezers to hold candy, dip half of each candy-coated chocolate into chocolate. Let dry on waxed paper. Attach chocolate-dipped and cinnamon candies to cookies using melted chocolate mixture (reheat if necessary) for eyes and nose of reindeers. Store in tightly covered container.

1 Cookie Pop: Calories 115; Total Fat 6g (Saturated Fat 3g, Trans Fat 0g); Cholesterol 15mg; Sodium 100mg; Total Carbohydrate 17g (Dietary Fiber 1g); Protein 2g **Exchanges:** 1 Starch, 1 Fat **Carbohydrate Choices:** 1

Chocolate Drop Cookies

PREP TIME: **50 Minutes** • START TO FINISH: **1 Hour 30 Minutes** • **About 3 dozen cookies**

COOKIES

1	cup granulated sugar
½	cup butter, softened
⅓	cup buttermilk
1	teaspoon vanilla
1	egg
2	oz unsweetened baking chocolate, melted, cooled
1¾	cups all-purpose flour
½	teaspoon baking soda
½	teaspoon salt

FROSTING

2	oz unsweetened baking chocolate
2	tablespoons butter
2	cups powdered sugar
3	tablespoons hot water

1. Heat oven to 400°F. Grease cookie sheet with shortening or cooking spray.

2. In large bowl, beat granulated sugar, ½ cup butter, the buttermilk, vanilla, egg and 2 oz melted chocolate with electric mixer on medium speed, or mix with spoon. Stir in flour, baking soda and salt.

3. On cookie sheet, drop dough by rounded tablespoonfuls about 2 inches apart.

4. Bake 8 to 10 minutes or until almost no indentation remains when touched in center. Immediately remove from cookie sheet to cooling rack. Cool completely, about 30 minutes.

5. In 2-quart saucepan, melt 2 oz chocolate and 2 tablespoons butter over low heat, stirring occasionally; remove from heat. Stir in powdered sugar and hot water until smooth. (If frosting is too thick, add more water, 1 teaspoon at a time. If frosting is too thin, add more powdered sugar, 1 tablespoon at a time.) Spread over cookies.

1 Cookie: Calories 120; Total Fat 5g (Saturated Fat 3g, Trans Fat 0g); Cholesterol 15mg; Sodium 80mg; Total Carbohydrate 18g (Dietary Fiber 0g); Protein 1g **Exchanges:** ½ Starch, ½ Other Carbohydrate, 1 Fat **Carbohydrate Choices:** 1

Tinsel Time Tips

Frost cookies with a container of your favorite flavor of ready-to-spread frosting instead of the homemade.

Store cookies in a tightly covered container with waxed paper between layers of cookies.

GLUTEN-FREE

Quick-Mix Chocolate Cookies

PREP TIME: 45 Minutes • **START TO FINISH:** 1 Hour 25 Minutes • **About 4 dozen cookies**

1   box Betty Crocker® Gluten Free devil's food cake mix

⅓   cup vegetable oil

1   teaspoon gluten-free vanilla

2   eggs

¼   cup sugar

1. Heat oven to 350°F. In large bowl, mix all ingredients except sugar with spoon until dough forms.

2. Shape dough into 48 (1-inch) balls; roll in sugar. On ungreased cookie sheets, place balls about 2 inches apart.

3. Bake 8 to 10 minutes or until set. Cool 1 minute; remove from cookie sheets to cooling racks. Cool completely, about 30 minutes. Store in tightly covered container.

1 Cookie: Calories 50; Total Fat 2g (Saturated Fat 0g, Trans Fat 0g); Cholesterol 10mg; Sodium 55mg; Total Carbohydrate 9g (Dietary Fiber 0g); Protein 0g **Exchanges:** ½ Other Carbohydrate, ½ Fat **Carbohydrate Choices:** ½

Chocolate–Chocolate Chip Cookies: Stir ⅔ cup miniature semisweet chocolate chips into the dough.

Tinsel Time Tips

For more sparkling cookies, roll dough balls in coarse sugar.

Cooking gluten free? Always read labels to make sure each recipe ingredient is gluten free. Products and ingredient sources can change.

Chocolate Hazelnut Cookies

PREP TIME: **1 Hour** • START TO FINISH: **1 Hour 45 Minutes** • **3 dozen cookies**

1   pouch Betty Crocker chocolate chip cookie mix

⅓   cup butter, softened

1   cup hazelnut spread with cocoa

1   egg

½   cup hazelnuts (filberts), toasted*, skins removed and nuts chopped

¾   cup white vanilla baking chips

2   teaspoons vegetable oil

1. Heat oven to 375°F. In large bowl stir cookie mix, butter, hazelnut spread and egg until soft dough forms. Stir in hazelnuts. Onto ungreased cookie sheets, drop dough by rounded teaspoonfuls 2 inches apart.

2. Bake 8 to 11 minutes or until edges are set. Cool 1 to 2 minutes; remove from cookie sheets to cooling racks. Cool completely.

3. In small bowl, place white chips and oil. Microwave on High 45 to 60 seconds, stirring every 25 seconds, until chips are melted and smooth. Spoon into small resealable food-storage plastic bag. Cut off tiny corner of bag. Squeeze bag to drizzle melted chips over cookies. Place on waxed paper. Let stand until set.

To toast hazelnuts, spread on ungreased cookie sheet. Bake at 375°F 8 to 10 minutes or until light golden brown. Cool slightly; place nuts in clean kitchen towel and rub vigorously to remove skins.

1 Cookie: Calories 160; Total Fat 8g (Saturated Fat 3.5g, Trans Fat 0g); Cholesterol 10mg; Sodium 80mg; Total Carbohydrate 19g (Dietary Fiber 0g); Protein 1g **Exchanges:** ½ Starch, 1 Other Carbohydrate, 1½ Fat **Carbohydrate Choices:** 1½

Holiday White Chocolate–Macaroon Cookies

PREP TIME: **30 Minutes** • START TO FINISH: **1 Hour** • **3 dozen cookies**

1 pouch Betty Crocker sugar cookie mix

½ cup butter, softened

1 egg

1 cup flaked coconut

1⅔ cups white vanilla baking chips

½ teaspoon coconut extract

1 teaspoon shortening

Red and green decorating sugars

Coarse white sparkling sugar

1. Heat oven to 375°F. In large bowl, stir cookie mix, butter, egg, coconut, 1 cup of the baking chips and the coconut extract until dough forms. Onto ungreased cookie sheets, drop dough by rounded teaspoonfuls 2 inches apart.

2. Bake 9 to 11 minutes or until golden brown around edges. Cool 1 minute; remove from cookie sheets to cooling racks. Cool completely, about 20 minutes.

3. In small microwavable bowl, microwave remaining ⅔ cup baking chips and the shortening on High 30 to 60 seconds or until mixture can be stirred smooth. Drizzle over cookies. Sprinkle with sugars as desired.

1 Cookie: Calories 150; Total Fat 8g (Saturated Fat 5g, Trans Fat 1g); Cholesterol 15mg; Sodium 80mg; Total Carbohydrate 19g (Dietary Fiber 0g); Protein 2g **Exchanges:** ½ Starch, 1 Other Carbohydrate, 1½ Fat **Carbohydrate Choices:** 1

Tinsel Time Tip

Keep cookies chewy and soft by storing them tightly covered. Resealable food-storage plastic bags, plastic food containers with tight-fitting lids and metal tins work best.

Decadent Double Chocolate–Cherry Cookies

PREP TIME: **1 Hour 10 Minutes** • START TO FINISH: **1 Hour 30 Minutes** • **32 cookies**

1 box Betty Crocker Gluten Free chocolate chip cookie mix

1 box (4-serving size) chocolate instant pudding and pie filling mix

1 cup dried cherries

½ cup coarsely chopped pecans

½ cup butter, melted

2 eggs

1 teaspoon gluten-free vanilla

1 cup semisweet chocolate chips (6 oz)

¼ cup whipping cream

1. Heat oven to 350°F. In large bowl, mix cookie mix, pudding mix, cherries and pecans. Add melted butter, eggs and vanilla; stir until soft dough forms.

2. Onto ungreased cookie sheets, drop dough by rounded tablespoonfuls; flatten slightly. Bake 9 to 11 minutes or until set. Cool 2 minutes; remove from cookie sheets to cooling racks. Cool completely.

3. Meanwhile, in small microwavable bowl, microwave chocolate chips and cream uncovered on High 30 to 45 seconds; stir until smooth. Spoon generous teaspoonful onto each cookie; spread over cookie. Let stand until chocolate is set, about 1 hour.

1 Cookie: Calories 190; Total Fat 8g (Saturated Fat 4g, Trans Fat 0g); Cholesterol 25mg; Sodium 150mg; Total Carbohydrate 26g (Dietary Fiber 0g); Protein 2g **Exchanges:** 1 Starch, 1 Other Carbohydrate, 1½ Fat **Carbohydrate Choices:** 2

Tinsel Time Tips

Cookies can be placed in a single layer in the refrigerator to make the chocolate frosting set up faster.

Cooking gluten free? Always read labels to make sure each recipe ingredient is gluten free. Products and ingredient sources can change.

Fudge Crinkles

PREP TIME: **45 Minutes** • START TO FINISH: **1 Hour 5 Minutes** • **3 dozen cookies**

1   box Betty Crocker Gluten Free devil's food cake mix

1   box (4-serving size) gluten-free chocolate instant pudding and pie filling mix

½   cup butter, melted

1   egg

¼   cup water

1   teaspoon gluten-free vanilla

    Sugar

1. Heat oven to 350°F. In large bowl, mix cake mix and pudding mix. Add melted butter, egg, water and vanilla; stir until soft dough forms.

2. In small bowl, place sugar. Shape dough into 36 (1¼-inch) balls; roll in sugar. On ungreased cookie sheets, place balls about 2 inches apart; flatten slightly.

3. Bake 8 to 10 minutes or until set. Cool 2 minutes; remove from cookie sheets to cooling racks. Cool completely, about 20 minutes. Store tightly covered.

1 Cookie: Calories 80; Total Fat 3g (Saturated Fat 2g, Trans Fat 0g); Cholesterol 15mg; Sodium 100mg; Total Carbohydrate 13g (Dietary Fiber 0g); Protein 0g **Exchanges:** 1 Other Carbohydrate, ½ Fat **Carbohydrate Choices:** 1

Tinsel Time Tip

Cooking gluten free? Always read labels to make sure each recipe ingredient is gluten free. Products and ingredient sources can change.

chapter
four

Bars & Brownies

Heavenly Chocolate Mousse Bars

PREP TIME: **30 Minutes** • START TO FINISH: **2 Hours 15 Minutes** • **36 bars**

1   pouch Betty Crocker sugar cookie mix

      Butter and egg called for on cookie mix pouch

1   bag (12 oz) semisweet chocolate chips (2 cups)

1   package (8 oz) cream cheese, softened

1½   cups whipping cream

1. Heat oven to 350°F. Mix cookie dough as directed on package, using butter and egg. Spread in bottom of ungreased 13x9-inch pan. Bake 12 to 15 minutes or until light golden brown. Cool in pan on cooling rack.

2. Meanwhile, in small microwavable bowl, microwave 1 cup of the chocolate chips uncovered on High 1 to 2 minutes, stirring once, until softened and chips can be stirred smooth. In medium bowl, beat cream cheese with electric mixer on medium speed until smooth. Add melted chocolate; stir until blended.

3. In small bowl, beat 1 cup of the whipping cream with electric mixer on high speed until stiff peaks form. Fold whipped cream into chocolate–cream cheese mixture until well blended. Spread over cooled cookie base. Cover; refrigerate 1 hour or until set.

4. In small microwavable bowl, microwave remaining 1 cup chocolate chips uncovered on High 1 to 2 minutes, stirring once, until softened and chips can be stirred smooth. Stir in remaining ½ cup whipping cream until blended. Spoon warm chocolate mixture over mousse layer; spread evenly. Refrigerate 30 minutes or until set. Cut into 9 rows by 4 rows. Store tightly covered in refrigerator.

1 Bar: Calories 180; Total Fat 12g (Saturated Fat 7g, Trans Fat 1g); Cholesterol 30mg; Sodium 85mg; Total Carbohydrate 17g (Dietary Fiber 0g); Protein 1g **Exchanges:** 1 Other Carbohydrate, 2½ Fat **Carbohydrate Choices:** 1

Chocolate–Peanut Butter Layer Bars

PREP TIME: **30 Minutes** • START TO FINISH: **2 Hours 25 Minutes** • **32 bars**

COOKIE BASE AND TOPPING

- 1 box Betty Crocker Gluten Free chocolate chip cookie mix
- ⅓ cup butter, softened
- ⅓ cup peanut butter
- 1 egg

FILLING

- 1¼ cups semisweet chocolate chips
- ¼ cup butter
- 1 package (8 oz) cream cheese, softened
- ⅔ cup peanut butter
- ¾ cup powdered sugar
- ½ cup whipping cream

1. Heat oven to 350°F. Spray bottom only of 13x9-inch pan with cooking spray. In large bowl, stir cookie base and topping ingredients until soft dough forms. Make 6 cookies by dropping rounded teaspoonfuls of dough onto ungreased cookie sheet; flatten slightly.

2. Press remaining dough in pan. Bake cookies and base 10 to 12 minutes or until edges are light golden brown. Cool 10 minutes. Reserve cookies for topping.

3. In small microwavable bowl, microwave chocolate chips and ¼ cup butter uncovered on High 1 minute to 1 minute 30 seconds, stirring every 30 seconds, until melted and stirred smooth. Spread evenly over bars. Refrigerate until firm, about 30 minutes.

4. In medium bowl, beat cream cheese, ⅔ cup peanut butter, the powdered sugar and whipping cream with electric mixer on low speed until blended. Beat on high speed about 2 minutes or until light and fluffy. Spread evenly over chocolate layer.

5. Crush reserved cookies; sprinkle over cream cheese layer. Press in lightly. Refrigerate until set, at least 1 hour. Cut into 8 rows by 4 rows. Store covered in refrigerator.

1 Bar: Calories 240; Total Fat 14g (Saturated Fat 7g, Trans Fat 0g); Cholesterol 25mg; Sodium 130mg; Total Carbohydrate 23g (Dietary Fiber 1g); Protein 3g **Exchanges:** 1 Starch, ½ Other Carbohydrate, 3 Fat **Carbohydrate Choices:** 1½

Tinsel Time Tip

Cooking gluten free? Always read labels to make sure each recipe ingredient is gluten free. Products and ingredient sources can change.

GLUTEN-FREE

Holiday Toffee Bars

PREP TIME: **15 Minutes** • START TO FINISH: **1 Hour 15 Minutes** • **32 bars**

1   cup butter, softened

1   cup packed brown sugar

1   teaspoon gluten-free vanilla

1   egg yolk

2   cups Bisquick Gluten Free mix

1   cup milk chocolate chips

½   cup chopped pecans or walnuts, if desired

1. Heat oven to 350°F. Spray 13x9-inch pan with cooking spray without flour. In large bowl, mix butter, brown sugar, vanilla and egg yolk. Stir in Bisquick mix. Press into pan.

2. Bake 20 to 25 minutes or until very light brown (crust will be soft). Immediately sprinkle chocolate chips over hot crust; let stand about 5 minutes or until chocolate is soft. Spread chocolate evenly; sprinkle with nuts. Cool in pan on cooling rack 30 minutes. Cut into 8 rows by 4 rows.

1 Bar: Calories 140; Total Fat 8g (Saturated Fat 4.5g, Trans Fat 0g); Cholesterol 25mg; Sodium 130mg; Total Carbohydrate 16g (Dietary Fiber 0g); Protein 1g **Exchanges:** ½ Starch, ½ Other Carbohydrate, 1½ Fat **Carbohydrate Choices:** 1

Tinsel Time Tips

Cooking gluten free? Always read labels to make sure each recipe ingredient is gluten free. Products and ingredient sources can change.

For the best results, cut the bars while they're still warm.

Holiday Eggnog Bars

PREP TIME: **15 Minutes** • START TO FINISH: **2 Hours 25 Minutes** • **36 bars**

½   cup butter, softened

¾   cup sugar

1   cup all-purpose flour

5   egg yolks

1¼ cups whipping cream

1   tablespoon rum or
    1 teaspoon rum extract

¾   teaspoon ground nutmeg

1. Heat oven to 350°F. Line bottom and sides of 9-inch square pan with foil so foil extends about 2 inches over 2 opposite sides of pan.

2. In small bowl, mix butter, ½ cup of the sugar and the flour. Press in bottom and ½ inch up sides of pan. Bake 20 minutes.

3. Reduce oven temperature to 300°F. In small bowl, beat egg yolks and remaining ¼ cup sugar with electric mixer on medium-high speed until thick. Gradually beat in whipping cream, rum and ¼ teaspoon of the nutmeg. Pour over partially baked crust.

4. Bake 40 to 50 minutes longer or until custard is set and knife inserted in center comes out clean. Cool completely in pan on cooling rack, about 1 hour.

5. Sprinkle tops of bars with remaining ½ teaspoon nutmeg. Use foil to lift out of pan. Cut into 6 rows by 6 rows. Store covered in refrigerator.

1 Bar: Calories 80; Total Fat 6g (Saturated Fat 4g, Trans Fat 0g); Cholesterol 45mg; Sodium 20mg; Total Carbohydrate 7g (Dietary Fiber 0g); Protein 1g **Exchanges:** ½ Other Carbohydrate, 1 Fat **Carbohydrate Choices:** ½

Tinsel Time Tip

Use an egg separator to easily separate the yolks from the egg whites.

Almond Streusel– Cherry Cheesecake Bars

PREP TIME: **45 Minutes** • START TO FINISH: **4 Hours** • **24 bars**

COOKIE BASE

- 1 pouch Betty Crocker sugar cookie mix
- ¼ cup cold butter
- 4 oz (half of 8-oz package) cream cheese

FILLING

- 2½ packages (8 oz each) cream cheese (20 oz), softened
- ½ cup sugar
- 2 tablespoons all-purpose flour
- 1 teaspoon almond extract
- 2 eggs
- 1 can (21 oz) cherry pie filling

TOPPING

- 1½ cups reserved cookie base mixture
- ½ cup sliced almonds

1. Heat oven to 350°F. Spray 13x9-inch pan with cooking spray.

2. Place cookie mix in large bowl. Cut in butter and 4 oz cream cheese, using pastry blender or fork, until mixture is crumbly. Reserve 1½ cups mixture for topping. Press remaining mixture in bottom of pan. Bake 12 minutes.

3. Meanwhile, in large bowl, beat 20 oz cream cheese, the sugar, flour, almond extract and eggs with electric mixer on medium speed until smooth.

4. Spread cream cheese mixture evenly over partially baked cookie base. Spoon pie filling evenly over cream cheese layer. Sprinkle with reserved cookie base mixture and the almonds.

5. Bake 40 to 45 minutes or until light golden brown. Cool 30 minutes. Refrigerate about 2 hours or until chilled. Cut into 6 rows by 4 rows. Store covered in refrigerator.

1 Bar: Calories 270; Total Fat 15g (Saturated Fat 8g, Trans Fat 1g); Cholesterol 55mg; Sodium 160mg; Total Carbohydrate 28g (Dietary Fiber 0g); Protein 4g **Exchanges:** 1 Starch, 1 Other Carbohydrate, 3 Fat **Carbohydrate Choices:** 2

Tinsel Time Tip

You'll need a total of 3 (8-ounce) packages of cream cheese for this recipe.

White Chocolate Cheesecake Bars

PREP TIME: **20 Minutes** • START TO FINISH: **4 Hours 20 Minutes** • **16 bars**

20 thin chocolate wafer cookies, crushed (1¼ cups)

6 tablespoons butter, melted

2 packages (8 oz each) cream cheese, softened

½ cup sugar

1 teaspoon vanilla

2 eggs

1 package (6 oz) white chocolate baking bars, chopped (1 cup)

1 tablespoon all-purpose flour

Fresh raspberries and mint leaves, if desired

1. Heat oven to 350°F. Grease 8-inch square pan with shortening or cooking spray. In small bowl, mix crushed cookies and butter. Press in bottom of pan. Bake 10 minutes. Cool completely, about 20 minutes.

2. Reduce oven temperature to 325°F. In large bowl, beat cream cheese, sugar and vanilla with electric mixer on medium speed until light and fluffy. Beat in eggs, one at a time, just until blended. In small bowl, mix chopped white chocolate and flour; fold into cream cheese mixture. Spread batter over crust.

3. Bake 28 to 30 minutes or until edges are set but center still jiggles slightly. Cool completely in pan on cooling rack, about 1 hour. Refrigerate 2 hours before serving. Cut into 4 rows by 4 rows. Garnish with raspberries and mint.

1 Bar: Calories 264; Total Fat 19g (Saturated Fat 11g); Sodium 205mg; Total Carbohydrate 20g (Dietary Fiber 0g); Protein 4g **Exchanges:** 1½ Other Carbohydrate, 3½ Fat **Carbohydrate Choices:** 1½

Strawberry Cheesecake Bars

PREP TIME: **15 Minutes** • START TO FINISH: **3 Hours 20 Minutes** • **32 bars**

1   pouch Betty Crocker sugar cookie mix

⅓   cup butter, melted

2   tablespoons all-purpose flour

3   eggs

2   packages (8 oz each) cream cheese, softened

¾   cup sugar

1   teaspoon vanilla

¾   cup strawberry spreadable fruit

1. Heat oven to 350°F. Spray bottom only of 13x9-inch pan with cooking spray.

2. In medium bowl, stir cookie mix, butter, flour and 1 of the eggs until soft dough forms. Press evenly in pan. Bake 15 to 18 minutes or until light golden brown. Cool 15 minutes.

3. In large bowl, beat cream cheese, sugar, vanilla and remaining 2 eggs with electric mixer on medium speed until smooth. Spread evenly over crust in pan.

4. Place spreadable fruit in small resealable food-storage plastic bag; seal bag. Cut off tiny corner of bag. Squeeze spreadable fruit in 3 lines the length of the pan. Use knife to pull spread from side to side through cream cheese mixture at 1-inch intervals.

5. Bake 25 to 30 minutes longer or until filling is set. Refrigerate until chilled, about 2 hours. Cut into 8 rows by 4 rows. Store covered in refrigerator.

1 Bar: Calories 180; Total Fat 9g (Saturated Fat 5g, Trans Fat 1g); Cholesterol 40mg; Sodium 100mg; Total Carbohydrate 22g (Dietary Fiber 0g); Protein 2g **Exchanges:** ½ Starch, 1 Other Carbohydrate, 2 Fat **Carbohydrate Choices:** 1½

Tinsel Time Tip

Add a new shape to your cookie tray. Cut bars diagonally in half to make triangles.

Baklava Bars

PREP TIME: **25 Minutes** • START TO FINISH: **2 Hours 50 Minutes** • **24 bars**

COOKIE BASE

- 1 pouch Betty Crocker sugar cookie mix
- ½ cup butter, softened
- ½ teaspoon grated lemon peel
- 1 egg

FILLING

- 1½ cups chopped walnuts
- ⅓ cup granulated sugar
- ¼ cup butter, softened
- 1 teaspoon ground cinnamon
- ⅛ teaspoon salt
- 8 frozen mini fillo shells (from 2.1-oz package)

GLAZE

- ⅓ cup honey
- 2 tablespoons butter, softened
- 1 tablespoon packed brown sugar
- ½ teaspoon lemon juice
- ¼ teaspoon ground cinnamon
- 1 teaspoon vanilla

GARNISH

- 4 tablespoons honey

1. Heat oven to 350°F. Spray bottom only of 13x9-inch pan with cooking spray.

2. In large bowl, stir cookie base ingredients until soft dough forms. Press in bottom of pan. Bake 15 minutes.

3. Meanwhile, in medium bowl, stir walnuts, granulated sugar, ¼ cup butter, 1 teaspoon cinnamon and the salt with fork until mixture is well mixed and crumbly.

4. Sprinkle nut mixture evenly over partially baked base. With hands, crumble frozen fillo shells evenly over nut mixture. Bake 18 to 20 minutes longer or until golden brown.

5. Meanwhile, in small microwavable bowl, microwave ⅓ cup honey, 2 tablespoons butter, the brown sugar, lemon juice and ¼ teaspoon cinnamon uncovered on High 1 minute or until bubbly. Stir in vanilla.

6. Drizzle glaze evenly over fillo. Cool completely, about 2 hours.

7. Cut into 6 rows by 4 rows. Before serving, drizzle about ½ teaspoon honey over each bar. Store covered at room temperature.

1 Bar: Calories 250; Total Fat 14g (Saturated Fat 5g, Trans Fat 1g); Cholesterol 25mg; Sodium 115mg; Total Carbohydrate 29g (Dietary Fiber 0g); Protein 2g **Exchanges:** ½ Starch, 1½ Other Carbohydrate, 2½ Fat **Carbohydrate Choices:** 2

Tinsel Time Tips

This was a prize-winning recipe in the 2007 Betty Crocker® Cookie Contest.

You can find mini fillo shells in the freezer section of your supermarket.

Cranberry-Macadamia Bars

PREP TIME: **30 Minutes** • START TO FINISH: **2 Hours** • **36 bars**

1 pouch Betty Crocker sugar cookie mix

⅓ cup butter, melted

1 egg

⅓ cup butter

¼ cup packed brown sugar

1 cup sweetened dried cranberries

1 cup macadamia nuts, coarsely chopped

½ cup white vanilla baking chips

1 teaspoon oil

1. Heat oven to 350°F. Grease 9-inch square pan with shortening or cooking spray.

2. In medium bowl, stir cookie mix, ⅓ cup melted butter and egg until soft dough forms. Press in bottom of pan. Bake 15 minutes.

3. In 1-quart saucepan, heat ⅓ cup butter, the brown sugar and cranberries to boiling over medium heat, stirring constantly. Spoon and spread cranberry mixture evenly over partially baked cookie base. Sprinkle with nuts.

4. Bake 10 to 15 minutes longer or until golden brown. Cool completely in pan on cooling rack, 1 hour.

5. In small rmicrowavable bowl, place baking chips and oil. Microwave on High 30 to 45 seconds, stirring every 20 seconds, until chips are melted and smooth. Spoon into small resealable food-storage plastic bag. Cut off tiny corner of bag; squeeze bag to drizzle over bars. Cut into 6 rows by 6 rows. Store tightly covered at room temperature.

1 Bar: Calories 130; Total Fat 7g (Saturated Fat 3.5g, Trans Fat 0.5g); Cholesterol 15mg; Sodium 65mg; Total Carbohydrate 15g (Dietary Fiber 0g); Protein 1g **Exchanges:** 1 Other Carbohydrate, 1½ Fat **Carbohydrate Choices:** 1

Chewy Raspberry-Almond Bars

PREP TIME: 20 Minutes • **START TO FINISH: 2 Hours** • **16 bars**

1½ cups quick-cooking oats

1½ cups all-purpose flour

¾ cup packed light brown sugar

½ teaspoon salt

¾ cup cold butter

1 egg, beaten

¾ cup seedless red raspberry jam

1 cup fresh raspberries (6 oz)

½ cup sliced almonds

1. Heat oven to 375°F. Spray 9-inch square pan with baking spray with flour.

2. In large bowl, mix oats, flour, brown sugar and salt. Cut in butter, using pastry blender or fork, until mixture looks like coarse crumbs. Reserve 1 cup mixture for topping. To remaining mixture, stir in egg until just moistened.

3. Using fingers or bottom of measuring cup, press dough firmly and evenly into bottom of pan. Spread evenly with jam. Arrange raspberries over jam. Stir almonds into reserved crumb mixture; sprinkle evenly over raspberries.

4. Bake 30 to 35 minutes or until top is golden. Cool 1 hour in pan on cooling rack. Cut into 4 rows by 4 rows.

1 Bar: Calories 260; Total Fat 11g (Saturated Fat 6g, Trans Fat 0g); Cholesterol 35mg; Sodium 150mg; Total Carbohydrate 36g (Dietary Fiber 2g); Protein 3g **Exchanges:** 2 Starch, ½ Other Carbohydrate, 1½ Fat **Carbohydrate Choices:** 2½

Chewy Blueberry-Almond Bars: Substitute fresh blueberries for the raspberries and blueberry preserves for the raspberry jam.

Tinsel Time Tip

If you don't have baking spray with flour, grease the pan with cooking spray and sprinkle lightly with flour.

Elegant Almond Bars

PREP TIME: **25 Minutes** • START TO FINISH: **2 Hours 30 Minutes** • **32 bars**

COOKIE BASE

1 pouch Betty Crocker sugar cookie mix

½ cup butter, melted

½ teaspoon almond extract

1 egg

FILLING

1 can (8 oz) or 1 package (7 oz) almond paste, crumbled into ½-inch pieces

¼ cup sugar

¼ cup butter, melted

2 eggs

½ cup sliced almonds

TOPPING

2 oz white chocolate baking bar, coarsely chopped (⅓ cup)

2 tablespoons shortening

¼ cup sliced almonds

1. Heat oven to 350°F. In large bowl, stir cookie base ingredients until soft dough forms. Spread in ungreased 13x9-inch pan. Bake 15 to 18 minutes or until light golden brown.

2. Meanwhile, in large bowl, beat almond paste, sugar and ¼ cup melted butter with electric mixer on low speed until blended. Add 2 eggs; beat until well blended (mixture may be slightly lumpy).

3. Spread almond paste mixture over partially baked base. Sprinkle with ½ cup almonds. Bake 15 to 20 minutes longer or until filling is set (filling will puff up during baking). Cool completely, about 1 hour.

4. In 1-quart heavy saucepan, melt white chocolate and shortening over low heat, stirring constantly, until smooth. Pour and spread over cooled bars. Sprinkle with ¼ cup almonds. Let stand about 30 minutes or until topping is set. Cut into 8 rows by 4 rows. Store covered at room temperature.

1 Bar: Calories 180; Total Fat 10g (Saturated Fat 4g, Trans Fat 1g); Cholesterol 30mg; Sodium 75mg; Total Carbohydrate 19g (Dietary Fiber 0g); Protein 3g **Exchanges:** 1½ Other Carbohydrate, ½ High-Fat Meat, 1 Fat **Carbohydrate Choices:** 1

Tinsel Time Tip

Alice Marshall, of San Luis Obispo, California, was a winner with this recipe in the 2007 Mix It Up with Betty! Cookie Mix Recipe Contest.

Fig-Walnut Gingerbread Bars

PREP TIME: **15 Minutes** • START TO FINISH: **3 Hours** • **16 bars**

1 pouch Betty Crocker gingerbread cookie mix

½ cup butter, softened

1 egg

1 jar (11.5 oz) fig preserves

½ cup chopped dried Calimyrna figs

2 tablespoons packed brown sugar

½ cup chopped walnuts, toasted*

Powdered sugar, if desired

1. Heat oven to 350°F. Line 8-inch square pan with foil, leaving foil overhanging at 2 opposite sides of pan; spray foil with cooking spray.

2. In large bowl, stir cookie mix, butter and egg until soft dough forms. Reserve ⅔ cup dough. Press remaining dough in bottom of pan. Bake 15 minutes.

3. In small bowl, mix preserves, figs and brown sugar. Spread over partially baked crust. Stir walnuts into reserved dough; crumble over filling.

4. Bake 30 to 32 minutes or until golden. Cool completely in pan on cooling rack, about 2 hours. Use foil to lift out of pan. Cut into 4 rows by 4 rows. Sprinkle with powdered sugar.

To toast walnuts, bake in ungreased shallow pan at 350°F for 6 to 10 minutes, stirring occasionally, until light brown.

1 Bar: Calories 275; Total Fat 11g (Saturated Fat 5g, Trans Fat 0g); Cholesterol 0mg; Sodium 269mg; Total Carbohydrate 41g (Dietary Fiber 1g); Protein 3g **Exchanges:** ½ Starch, 2 Other Carbohydrate, 2 Fat **Carbohydrate Choices:** 2½

Tinsel Time Tips

Gingerbread cookie mix brings a wonderful holiday spice flavor to these gooey fig bars. Look for the cookie mix at holiday time—it's only available for a short time each year!

We used Calimyrna figs in this recipe because we like their distinctive sweet, nutty flavor and golden color, but you could use any other variety of dried figs that you have on hand.

Nutty Noel Bars

PREP TIME: **15 Minutes** • START TO FINISH: **1 Hour 35 Minutes** • **32 bars**

1½	cups Original Bisquick mix
1	cup old-fashioned or quick-cooking oats
¾	cup packed brown sugar
⅓	cup butter, softened
1	egg
1¼	cups white baking chips
2	tablespoons whipping cream
1½	cups mixed nuts or cashews

1. Heat oven to 350°F. Lightly grease bottom only of 13x9-inch pan with shortening or spray bottom with cooking spray.

2. In large bowl, stir Bisquick mix, oats, brown sugar, butter and egg until well blended. Press in bottom of pan. Bake 16 to 18 minutes or until golden brown.

3. In small microwavable bowl, place white baking chips and whipping cream. Microwave uncovered on Medium-High (70%) 1 minute; stir. Microwave 10 to 15 seconds longer or until mixture can be stirred smooth. Spread over baked layer. Sprinkle with nuts; press gently into topping. Cool completely, about 1 hour. Cut into 8 rows by 4 rows.

1 Cookie: Calories 170; Total Fat 10g (Saturated Fat 4.5g, Trans Fat 0g); Cholesterol 15mg; Sodium 105mg; Total Carbohydrate 18g (Dietary Fiber 0g); Protein 2g **Exchanges:** ½ Starch, ½ Other Carbohydrate, 2 Fat **Carbohydrate Choices:** 1

Tinsel Time Tip

There's a treasure chest of goodness in these sweet and salty nutty bars. You can use salted pecan halves or peanuts in place of the mixed nuts. Keep bars tightly covered at room temperature, or freeze up to 3 months.

Salted Caramel Turtle Triangles

PREP TIME: **20 Minutes** • START TO FINISH: **1 Hour 30 Minutes** • **48 bars**

COOKIE BASE

1   pouch Betty Crocker double chocolate chunk cookie mix

¼   cup butter, melted

2   tablespoons water

1   egg

⅔   cup pecans, coarsely chopped

TOPPING

4   tablespoons butter

1   bag (14 oz) caramels (about 50 caramels)

¼   cup whipping cream

½   teaspoon vanilla

⅛   teaspoon coarse kosher salt, plus additional ½ teaspoon for top of bars

1. Heat oven to 350°F. Spray 13x9-inch pan with cooking spray. In medium bowl, stir cookie mix, ¼ cup melted butter, the water and egg until soft dough forms.

2. Press dough evenly into pan, sprinkle with ⅓ cup of the pecans. Bake 11 to 15 minutes or until set in center and edges just begin to pull from sides of pan. Set aside to cool.

3. Meanwhile, in medium saucepan over medium-low heat, melt 4 tablespoons butter, the caramels and cream, stirring frequently until mixture is smooth. Remove from heat. Stir in vanilla and ⅛ teaspoon salt.

4. Spread caramel mixture evenly over cookie base; sprinkle with remaining ⅓ cup pecans. Cool completely. Sprinkle with additional salt right before serving. Cut into 4 rows by 6 rows; cut each square diagonally into triangles. Store in refrigerator; bring to room temperature before serving.

1 Bar: Calories 110; Total Fat 5g (Saturated Fat 2.5g, Trans Fat 0g); Cholesterol 15mg; Sodium 110mg; Total Carbohydrate 15g (Dietary Fiber 0g); Protein 1g **Exchanges:** 1 Other Carbohydrate, 1 Fat **Carbohydrate Choices:** 1

Tinsel Time Tip

To use as a holiday gift, layer in a gift box or tin with parchment paper between layers.

Butter Pecan Chews

PREP TIME: **20 Minutes** • START TO FINISH: **2 Hours 35 Minutes** • **36 bars**

1½ cups all purpose flour

3 tablespoons granulated sugar

¾ cup butter, softened

3 eggs, separated

2½ cups packed light brown sugar

1 teaspoon vanilla

½ teaspoon salt

1 cup chopped pecans

¾ cup flaked coconut

2 tablespoons powdered sugar

1. Heat oven to 375°F. Grease 13x9-inch pan with butter.

2. In medium bowl, mix flour, granulated sugar and butter. Press mixture in bottom of pan. Bake 12 to 14 minutes or until light brown.

3. Meanwhile, in large bowl, beat egg yolks, brown sugar, vanilla and salt with electric mixer until well blended. Stir in pecans and coconut. In small bowl, beat egg whites with electric mixer until foamy. Fold into egg yolk mixture.

4. Spread filling evenly over partially baked crust. Reduce oven temperature to 350°F.

5. Bake 25 to 30 minutes longer or until deep golden brown and center is set. Sprinkle with powdered sugar. Cool in pan on cooling rack 30 minutes. Cut into 6 rows by 6 rows.

1 Bar: Calories 160; Total Fat 7g (Saturated Fat 3.5g, Trans Fat 0g); Cholesterol 30mg; Sodium 75mg; Total Carbohydrate 22g (Dietary Fiber 0g); Protein 1g **Exchanges:** 1½ Other Carbohydrate, 1½ Fat **Carbohydrate Choices:** 1½

Tinsel Time Tips

With a flavor like pecan pie, these rich and buttery bars are perfect for any holiday gathering and would also be a fabulous gift!

These were created by Holiday Cookie Contest Winner Lisa Chambers.

Mint Cheesecake Squares

PREP TIME: **30 Minutes** • START TO FINISH: **4 Hours** • **20 bars**

CRUST

1   package (9 oz) thin chocolate wafer cookies, crushed (1¾ cups)

½   cup butter, melted

FILLING

2   packages (8 oz) cream cheese, softened

½   cup sour cream

4   eggs

⅔   cup sugar

½   cup crème de menthe syrup

¼   teaspoon mint extract

TOPPING

4   oz semisweet baking chocolate, chopped

½   cup sour cream

1. Heat oven to 350°F. In medium bowl, mix crust ingredients. Press in bottom of ungreased 13x9-inch pan. Freeze crust while preparing filling.

2. In large bowl, beat filling ingredients with electric mixer on low speed until smooth. Pour into crust-lined pan. Bake 30 to 35 minutes or until knife inserted in center comes out clean. Cool in pan on cooling rack.

3. Meanwhile, in 1-quart saucepan, melt chocolate over low heat, stirring constantly. Cool 5 minutes. Beat in sour cream with spoon. Spread over warm cheesecake. Refrigerate 3 hours or until firm. Cut into 5 rows by 4 rows. Store in refrigerator.

1 Bar: Calories 300; Total Fat 21g (Saturated Fat 10g, Trans Fat 2g); Cholesterol 75mg; Sodium 220mg; Total Carbohydrate 25g (Dietary Fiber 1g); Protein 5g **Exchanges:** ½ Starch, 1 Other Carbohydrate, ½ Medium-Fat Meat, 3½ Fat **Carbohydrate Choices:** 1½

Tinsel Time Tip

You can make these bars up to 2 days ahead of time. Store them in the refrigerator.

Peppermint Patty Brownies

PREP TIME: **20 Minutes** • START TO FINISH: **1 Hour 50 Minutes** • **16 brownies**

1   box Betty Crocker® Gluten Free brownie mix

¼   cup butter, melted

2   eggs

½   cup sweetened condensed milk (not evaporated)

1½   teaspoons pure peppermint extract

2½   to 3 cups powdered sugar

1   cup chocolate creamy ready-to-spread frosting (from 1-lb container)

1. Heat oven to 350°F (325°F for dark or nonstick pan). Line 8- or 9-inch square pan with foil so foil extends about 2 inches over 2 opposite sides of pan. Grease bottom only of foil with shortening.

2. In medium bowl, stir brownie mix, butter and eggs until well blended (batter will be thick). Spread in pan.

3. Bake 8-inch pan 28 to 31 minutes, 9-inch pan 26 to 30 minutes, or until toothpick inserted 2 inches from side of pan comes out almost clean. Cool completely, about 1 hour.

4. In medium bowl, stir condensed milk and peppermint extract. Beat in enough powdered sugar with electric mixer on low speed until blended and slightly crumbly. Turn out onto surface sprinkled with powdered sugar; knead lightly to form a smooth ball. Pat mixture evenly over top of brownies.

5. Remove brownies from pan by lifting foil. Spread frosting over brownies. Cut into 4 rows by 4 rows.

1 Brownie: Calories 330; Total Fat 9g (Saturated Fat 4.5g, Trans Fat 1g); Cholesterol 35mg; Sodium 150mg; Total Carbohydrate 59g (Dietary Fiber 1g); Protein 2g **Exchanges:** ½ Starch, 3½ Other Carbohydrate, 2 Fat **Carbohydrate Choices:** 4

Tinsel Time Tips

Sprinkle frosted brownies with crushed peppermint candies or chopped thin mints.

Cooking gluten free? Always read labels to make sure each recipe ingredient is gluten free. Products and ingredient sources can change.

Traditional Holiday Tree Brownies

PREP TIME: **30 Minutes** • START TO FINISH: **2 Hours** • **21 brownies**

1 box Betty Crocker® fudge brownie mix

Water, vegetable oil and eggs called for on brownie mix box

1 cup vanilla creamy ready-to-spread frosting (from 1-lb container)

2 to 3 drops green food color

Red and green candy sprinkles or miniature candy-coated chocolate baking bits

Miniature candy canes (2 inch), unwrapped

1. Heat oven to 350°F. Line 13x9-inch pan with foil so foil extends about 2 inches over short sides of pan. Grease bottom only of foil with cooking spray or shortening.

2. Make and bake brownie mix as directed on box for 13x9-inch pan, using water, oil and eggs. Cool completely, about 1 hour. Remove brownie from pan by lifting foil; peel foil away. To cut brownie into triangles, cut lengthwise into 3 rows. Cut each row into 7 triangles; see diagram. Save smaller pieces for snacking.

3. In small bowl, place frosting; stir food color into frosting. Spoon frosting into small resealable food-storage plastic bag; seal bag. Cut off tiny corner of bag. Squeeze bag to pipe frosting over brownies. Sprinkle with candy sprinkles.

4. Break off curved ends of candy canes. Insert 1 straight piece into bottom of each triangle to make tree trunk.

1 Brownie: Calories 240; Total Fat 8g (Saturated Fat 3g, Trans Fat 1g); Cholesterol 10mg; Sodium 120mg; Total Carbohydrate 39g (Dietary Fiber 1g); Protein 1g **Exchanges:** ½ Starch, 2 Other Carbohydrate, 1½ Fat **Carbohydrate Choices:** 2½

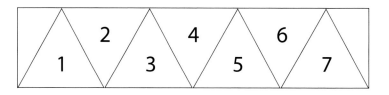

Bourbon-Spiked Brownie Truffle Balls

PREP TIME: **35 Minutes** • START TO FINISH: **2 Hours** • **About 60 truffle balls**

BROWNIES

1 box Betty Crocker fudge brownie mix

⅔ cup butter, melted

3 eggs

½ cup miniature semisweet chocolate chips

½ cup bourbon

½ teaspoon ground ginger

2 cups crushed gingersnap cookies (about 40 cookies)

GARNISH, IF DESIRED

½ cup powdered sugar or unsweetened baking cocoa

½ cup white baking chips or semisweet chocolate chips, melted

½ cup finely chopped crystallized ginger

1. Heat oven to 350°F. Spray bottom only of 13x9-inch pan with cooking spray.

2. In medium bowl, mix brownie mix, melted butter, eggs, ½ cup miniature chocolate chips, ¼ cup of the bourbon, the ground ginger and crushed cookies until well blended. Spread in pan.

3. Bake 24 to 26 minutes or until toothpick inserted 2 inches from side of pan comes out clean. Cool completely, about 1 hour. In medium bowl, crumble cooled brownie into chunks; stir in remaining ¼ cup bourbon. Shape mixture into 60 (1-inch) balls.

4. In small bowl, place ½ cup powdered sugar. Roll balls in powdered sugar. Drizzle or coat with melted white baking chips or semisweet chocolate chips and garnish with crystallized ginger. Store tightly covered in refrigerator up to 1 week or in freezer up to 1 month.

1 Truffle Ball: Calories 80; Total Fat 3.5g (Saturated Fat 1.5g, Trans Fat 0g); Cholesterol 15mg; Sodium 75mg; Total Carbohydrate 12g (Dietary Fiber 0g); Protein 0g **Exchanges:** ½ Starch, ½ Other Carbohydrate, ½ Fat **Carbohydrate Choices:** 1

Tinsel Time Tips

Brownies can be made ahead and stored in an airtight container at room temperature up to 2 days or in freezer up to 1 month. Then all you have to do on serving day is roll and coat the truffle balls.

For a festive touch, serve in shot glasses or small cupcake liners.

Ultimate Holiday Brownies

PREP TIME: **15 Minutes** • START TO FINISH: **2 Hours** • **16 brownies**

1   box Betty Crocker® Original Supreme Premium brownie mix

   Water, oil and egg called for on brownie mix box

1   cup plus 2 tablespoons creamy white ready-to-spread frosting (from 1-lb container)

⅛   to ¼ teaspoon mint or peppermint extract

   Green or pink food color

   Peppermint or spearmint candies, crushed, if desired

1. Heat oven to 350°F (325°F for dark or nonstick pan). Grease bottom only of 8-inch or 9-inch square pan with cooking spray or shortening. Make and bake brownies as directed on box, using water, oil and egg. Cool completely, about 1 hour.

2. In small bowl, stir frosting, extract and food color until smooth. Spread over brownies. Sprinkle with crushed candies. Cut into 4 rows by 4 rows. Store tightly covered.

1 Brownie: Calories 240; Total Fat 8g (Saturated Fat 1.5g, Trans Fat 1g); Cholesterol 15mg; Sodium 150mg; Total Carbohydrate 40g (Dietary Fiber 1g); Protein 1g **Exchanges:** ½ Starch, 2 Other Carbohydrate, 1½ Fat **Carbohydrate Choices:** 2½

Tinsel Time Tip

Cut brownies into bite-size pieces and serve in holiday paper liners for easy dessert pickups.

Whoopie Pie Brownies

PREP TIME: **20 Minutes** • START TO FINISH: **2 Hours 25 Minutes** • **16 brownies**

BROWNIES

1	box Betty Crocker Gluten Free brownie mix
¼	cup butter, melted
2	eggs

TOPPING

1	cup powdered sugar
½	cup butter, softened
1	cup marshmallow creme (from 7- or 13-oz jar)
1	teaspoon gluten-free vanilla
¼	cup semisweet chocolate chips

1. Heat oven to 350°F (325°F for dark or nonstick pan). Spray bottom only of 8- or 9-inch square pan with cooking spray (without flour).

2. In medium bowl, stir brownie mix, ¼ cup butter and the eggs until well blended (batter will be thick). Spread in pan.

3. Bake 8-inch pan 28 to 31 minutes, 9-inch pan 26 to 30 minutes, or until toothpick inserted 2 inches from side of pan comes out almost clean. Cool completely, about 1 hour.

4. In medium bowl, beat powdered sugar and ½ cup butter with electric mixer on medium speed until light and fluffy. On low speed, beat in marshmallow creme and vanilla until combined. Spread over brownies.

5. In small microwavable bowl, place chocolate chips. Microwave on High 30 to 60 seconds, stirring every 15 seconds, until chocolate is melted and smooth. Spoon into small resealable food-storage plastic bag. Cut off tiny corner of bag; squeeze bag to drizzle chocolate over brownies. Let stand 30 minutes or until chocolate is set. Cut into 4 rows by 4 rows. Store loosely covered at room temperature.

1 Brownie: Calories 270; Total Fat 12g (Saturated Fat 7g, Trans Fat 0g); Cholesterol 50mg; Sodium 135mg; Total Carbohydrate 38g (Dietary Fiber 1g); Protein 2g **Exchanges:** ½ Starch, 2 Other Carbohydrate, 2½ Fat **Carbohydrate Choices:** 2½

Tinsel Time Tips

An offset, thin metal spatula can be a cook's best friend. Use it in this recipe to spread brownie batter evenly in pan and to spread the topping over the baked brownies.

Cooking gluten free? Always read labels to make sure each recipe ingredient is gluten free. Products and ingredient sources can change.

Metric Conversion Guide

Note: The recipes in this cookbook have not been developed or tested using metric measures. When converting recipes to metric, some variations in quality may be noted.

Volume

U.S. Units	Canadian Metric	Australian Metric
¼ teaspoon	1 mL	1 ml
½ teaspoon	2 mL	2 ml
1 teaspoon	5 mL	5 ml
1 tablespoon	15 mL	20 ml
¼ cup	50 mL	60 ml
⅓ cup	75 mL	80 ml
½ cup	125 mL	125 ml
⅔ cup	150 mL	170 ml
¾ cup	175 mL	190 ml
1 cup	250 mL	250 ml
1 quart	1 liter	1 liter
1½ quarts	1.5 liters	1.5 liters
2 quarts	2 liters	2 liters
2½ quarts	2.5 liters	2.5 liters
3 quarts	3 liters	3 liters
4 quarts	4 liters	4 liters

Weight

U.S. Units	Canadian Metric	Australian Metric
1 ounce	30 grams	30 grams
2 ounces	55 grams	60 grams
3 ounces	85 grams	90 grams
4 ounces (¼ pound)	115 grams	125 grams
8 ounces (½ pound)	225 grams	225 grams
16 ounces (1 pound)	455 grams	500 grams
1 pound	455 grams	0.5 kilogram

Measurements

Inches	Centimeters
1	2.5
2	5.0
3	7.5
4	10.0
5	12.5
6	15.0
7	17.5
8	20.5
9	23.0
10	25.5
11	28.0
12	30.5
13	33.0

Temperatures

Fahrenheit	Celsius
32°	0°
212°	100°
250°	120°
275°	140°
300°	150°
325°	160°
350°	180°
375°	190°
400°	200°
425°	220°
450°	230°
475°	240°
500°	260°

Recipe Testing and Calculating Nutrition Information

Recipe Testing:

- Large eggs and 2% milk were used unless otherwise indicated.

- Fat-free, low-fat, low-sodium or lite products were not used unless indicated.

- No nonstick cookware and bakeware were used unless otherwise indicated. No dark-colored, black or insulated bakeware was used.

- When a pan is specified, a metal pan was used; a baking dish or pie plate means ovenproof glass was used.

- An electric hand mixer was used for mixing only when mixer speeds are specified.

Calculating Nutrition:

- The first ingredient was used wherever a choice is given, such as 1/3 cup sour cream or plain yogurt.

- The first amount was used wherever a range is given, such as 3- to 3½-pound whole chicken.

- The first serving number was used wherever a range is given, such as 4 to 6 servings.

- "If desired" ingredients were not included.

- Only the amount of a marinade or frying oil that is absorbed was included.

Index

Page numbers in *italics* indicate illustrations

H

Hazelnut
Chocolate Cookies, 150, *151*
Linzer Cookies, 38, *39*
–Peanut Butter Sandwich Cookies, 44, *45*
Truffles, Baked, 136, *137*
Heavenly Chocolate Mousse Bars, 160, *161*
Holiday Cookie Ornaments, 76, *77*
Holiday Cutouts, 70, *71*
Holiday Eggnog Bars, 166, *167*
Holiday House Cookies, 84, *85*
Holiday Snickerdoodles, 124, *125*
Holiday Surprise Sugar Cookies, 14, *15*
Holiday Toffee Bars, 164, *165*
Holiday White Chocolate–Macaroon Cookies, 152, *153*
House Cookies, Holiday, 84, *85*

I–J

Italian Pignoli Nut Cookies, 130, *131*

Jolly Snowman Faces, 108, *109*

L

Lemon
-Ginger Delights, 122, *123*
Snowdrops, 40, *41*
Snowflakes, Sparkling, 88, *89*
Lime Christmas Wreaths, 90, *91*
Linzer Cookies, 38, *39*
Almond, 36, *37*

M

Macadamia-Cranberry Bars, 176, *177*
Macaroon–White Chocolate Cookies, Holiday, 152, *153*
Merry Molasses Cookies, 92, *93*
Mini Whoopie Pies, 54, *55*
Mint Cheesecake Squares, 190, *191*
Mittens, Snowflake, 66, *67*
Molasses Cookies, Merry, 92, *93*

N–O

Nutty Noel Bars, 184, *185*

Oatmeal Shortbread Santas, 82, *83*
Orange Snowdrops, 40
Ornaments, Holiday Cookie, 76, *77*

P

Peanut Butter
Blossom Cookies, Festive, 142, *143*
–Chocolate Layer Bars, 162, *163*
Cookie Cups, 34, *35*
Cookies, Fudge-Filled, 48, *49*
–Hazelnut Sandwich Cookies, 44, *45*
Reindeer Cookies, 140, *141*
Reindeer Pops, 144, *145*
Pecan(s)
Butter Pecan Chews, 188, *189*
-Shortbread Trees, 120, *121*
Peppermint
Brownies, Peppermint Patty, 192, *193*
Candy Cookies, Easy, 106, *107*
Candy Tartlets, 26, *27*
Chocolate Tartlets, 28, *29*
Striped Peppermint Cookies, 114, *115*
Whoopie Pies, Pink, 50
Pignoli Nut Cookies, Italian, 130, *131*
Pink Peppermint Whoopie Pies, 50
Pinwheels, Chocolate-Cherry, 112, *113*
Pistachio-Raspberry Thumbprints, 20, *21*
Poinsettia Blossoms, Raspberry, 98, *99*
Pops. *See* Cookie Pops
Porcelain Cookies, 68, *69*

Q–R

Quick-Mix Chocolate Cookies, 148, *149*
Raspberry
-Almond Bars, Chewy, 178, *179*
-Pistachio Thumbprints, 20, *21*
Poinsettia Blossoms, 98, *99*
Ribbon Slices, 22, *23*
Red Velvet Rich-and-Creamy Cookies, 110, *111*

Complete your cookbook library with these *Betty Crocker* titles

Betty Crocker 30-Minute Meals for Diabetes

Betty Crocker The 300 Calorie Cookbook

Betty Crocker The 1500 Calorie a Day Cookbook

Betty Crocker Baking Basics

Betty Crocker's Best Bread Machine Cookbook

Betty Crocker's Best-Loved Recipes

Betty Crocker The Big Book of Bisquick®

Betty Crocker The Big Book of Cakes

Betty Crocker The Big Book of Cookies

Betty Crocker The Big Book of Cupcakes

Betty Crocker The Big Book of Pies and Tarts

Betty Crocker The Big Book of Slow Cooker, Casseroles & More

Betty Crocker The Big Book of Weeknight Dinners

Betty Crocker Bisquick® II Cookbook

Betty Crocker Bisquick® Impossibly Easy Pies

Betty Crocker Bisquick® to the Rescue

Betty Crocker Christmas Cookbook

Betty Crocker's Cook Book for Boys and Girls

Betty Crocker Cookbook, 11th Edition— The **BIG RED** *Cookbook*®

Betty Crocker Cookbook, Bridal Edition

Betty Crocker's Cooking Basics

Betty Crocker's Cooky Book, Facsimile Edition

Betty Crocker Decorating Cakes and Cupcakes

Betty Crocker Diabetes Cookbook

Betty Crocker's Easy Slow Cooker Dinners

Betty Crocker Fix-with-a-Mix Desserts

Betty Crocker Gluten-Free Cooking

Betty Crocker Grilling Made Easy

Betty Crocker Halloween Cookbook

Betty Crocker Healthy Heart Cookbook

Betty Crocker Indian Home Cooking

Betty Crocker Kids Cook!

Betty Crocker Living with Cancer Cookbook

Betty Crocker Money Saving Meals

Betty Crocker More Slow Cooker Recipes

Betty Crocker One-Dish Meals

Betty Crocker's Picture Cook Book, Facsimile Edition

Betty Crocker Quick & Easy Cookbook

Betty Crocker's Slow Cooker Cookbook

Betty Crocker Ultimate Bisquick® Cookbook

Betty Crocker Vegetarian Cooking

Betty Crocker Whole Grains

DISCARD NT PLEASANT